REAGAN: AMERICAN ICON

Robert Metzger

A Center Gallery Publication
Bucknell University

1989

Distributed by
University of Pennsylvania Press

This book is published in conjunction with an exhibition of the same title organized by the Center Gallery of Bucknell University, Lewisburg, Pennsylvania 17837 from January 14 through March 23, 1989, and circulated to Humphrey Fine Art, New York City, from May 3 through June 11, 1989 and to the Reading Public Museum and Art Gallery, Reading, Pennsylvania from June 25 through August 10, 1989.

The exhibition is supported in part by grants from the Pennsylvania Council on the Arts and the Association for the Arts, Bucknell University.

Library of Congress Catalogue-in-Publication Data

Metzger, Robert P.
    Reagan: American Icon

Bibliography: p.

1. Ronald Wilson Reagan, b. 1911. 2. Painters and sculptors — United States — Biography. 3. Nancy Davis (Reagan) — Motion picture and television credits. I. Ronald Wilson Reagan, b. 1911. II. Metzger, Robert Paul. III. Bucknell University, Center Gallery. IV. Title.

89-060966
ISBN 0-8122-8211-6 (cloth)
ISBN 0-8122-1302-5 (paper)

Distributed by University of Pennsylvania Press
Blockley Hall, 13th Floor
418 Service Drive
Philadelphia, PA 19104

Book produced by Phase One Graphic Resources;
    Ric Jones, designer.

Printed in the United States of America.

On the cover: Komar & Melamid, *Portrait of Ronald Reagan as Centaur, 1981,* Oil on canvas, 91 x 63, Michael H. Steinhardt.

C O N T E N T S

A R T I S T S

Robert Arneson

Edward Brezinski

Roger Brown

Nancy Burson

Andrew Castrucci

Richard Clarke

Peter Cole

Robbie Conal

Jeffrey Drieblatt

Jimmy Ernst

Mike Glier

Sidney Goodman

Red Grooms

Hans Haacke

William L. Haney

Ori Hofmekler

Sandy Huffaker

Alfredo Jaar

Jerry Kearns

Komar & Melamid

Alexander Kosalapov

Edward Larson

Alfred Leslie

Paul Marcus

Leon McFadden

Wit McKay

Marilyn Minter

Dimitri Prigov

Tim Rollins & K.O.S.
    (Kids of Survival)

David Sandlin

Peter Saul

Valerie Sivilli

Gregg Smith

Anton Van Dalen

Stephen Verona

Andy Warhol

Weegee (Arthur Felling)

David Wojnarowicz

L E N D E R S

Dr. and Mrs. Stanley B. Becker

Robert Berman Gallery

The Bertrand Library

Diane Brown Gallery

Capricorn Galleries

Andrew Castrucci

Richard Clarke

Terry Dintenfass Gallery

Bill Dobbs

Jeffrey M. Drieblatt

George Dudley

Dallas Ernst

Exit Art

Ronald Feldman Fine Art

Marc Filippone

Frumkin/Adams Gallery

Mike Glier

Nada Gray

Kurt Ilgen

George Jenks

Kent Fine Art, Inc.

Phyllis Kind Gallery, Inc.

Alexander Kosolapov

Robert Lehmann

Robert and Mary Looker

Bates Lowry

Edward Maloney

Gracie Mansion Gallery

Marlborough Gallery

Wit McKay

Marilyn Minter

Jose Mussavi Gallery

National Portrait Gallery

P.P.O.W.

Rosalyn Richards

Alfred and Virginia Silbowitz

Gilbert and Lila Silverman

Valerie A. Sivilli

Paul Slansky

Gregg Smith

Holly Solomon Gallery

Michael Steinhardt

Struve Gallery

Stephen Verona

John Weber Gallery

Lawrence S. Wilkinson

Melvin D. Wolf

Zolla/Lieberman Gallery

P R E F A C E

This volume is a documentation of the first comprehensive exhibition devoted to a sitting American president by a wide-ranging cross section of prominent painters and sculptors. The selection of artists was objective, apolitical and, we hope, representative of the great diversity and creative richness of American art in the decade of the 1980s.

Never before in the history of the nation has a president of the United States stimulated the imagination of such a large number of mainstream artists to achieve works of the highest aesthetic level. The majority of artists in the exhibition are not portraitists per se, but rather painters and sculptors whose virtuosity of expression is truly magnanimous. The latitude of feeling toward the subject of their art is incredibly broad, ranging from the reverential to the critical, with humor as a leitmotif running throughout the works in the exhibition. These works provide fresh insight and expand our perceptions of the man and the office.

Unlike the centuries-old tradition of officially sanctioned monarchial and aristocratic portraiture in which the subjects were usually idealized or flattered, the democratic spirit of America has fostered a more spontaneous and varied tradition of unbridled visual expression and interpretation. It was in this American atmosphere of individual freedom that these authentic, powerful images were conceived and realized.

Since Hollywood has long functioned as the repository and disseminator of America's collective folklore and because of the unique origins of the physical look of both President Ronald Reagan and First Lady Nancy (Davis) Reagan in the American entertainment industry, special attention was paid to their Hollywood years. They became part of the public's daily life as actors decades before their emergence on the political scene. Their basic image was honed to perfection in Hollywood where they became the personification of the American dream. A comprehensive chronology, filmography, and televisionography, together with an extensive visual bibliography, is designed to place the subjects of the exhibition in a larger cultural perspective.

The efficaciousness of the Reagan countenance is due in part to the unusually long period of time in which that image has been placed before the public eye. For over fifty years an indelible visual, as well as auditory, imprint has been fixed on the American consciousness, conveyed through radio, film, magazines, newspapers, movie posters, postcards, T-shirts, product advertisements, political buttons, bumper stickers, billboards, books, and, most proficiently of all, through the medium of television. The pervasiveness and continuity of this mass media image, never out of public view from the 1930s through the 1980s, is unprecedented in constancy, repetitiousness, and sheer staying power as well as in its evolution. The faces of Ronald and Nancy Reagan are arguably the best known in modern times because of their omnipresent dual fame, which has stretched across the better part of the twentieth century.

Acknowledgments

Our sincere thanks to the many persons who cooperated and contributed to this ambitious effort. At Bucknell University, we are indebted to President Gary Sojka, Associate Provost Barbara Shailor, Center Gallery Assistant Cynthia Peltier and the following students: Mikki Delmonico, Steve Gongola, Tom Simmons, and Ann Stugrin. Our gratitude also for the significant contributions of Kay Bishop, Lennie Buff, Jean Carter, Nancy Cleaver, Deanna Congileo, Debra Cook, Beverly Cox, Cheryl Dolby, Caril Dreyfuss, Alan Fern, Marsha Scott Gori, Nada Gray, Peggy Harris, Connie Heddings, Richard Humphrey, James J. Hurley, Nancy Lenker, Miranda McGinnis, Brian O'Neill, Marc Pachter, Betsy Powers, Christopher Reynolds, Rosalyn Richards, Martin Sklar, Maureen O'Hara Smith, William Stapp, David Stephens, Robert G. Stewart, Allen Topolski, Nancy S. Weyant, and Martin Winkler.

The exhibition and catalogue were made possible by grants from the Pennsylvania Council on the Arts and the Association for the Arts, Bucknell University. I wish to thank the many generous lenders and the artists whose cooperation was fundamental to the realization of the exhibition.

R.P.M.

Reagan: American Icon

The basic image of President Ronald Wilson Reagan remains remarkably unchanged from that of Hollywood actor Ronald Reagan. The identity which he had carefully created in Hollywood merged uncannily with his Washington persona. The studio movie set metamorphosed into the oval office at 1600 Pennsylvania Avenue. There is no clear-cut separation between entertainment mass media and political-informational mass media, only one long, slow dissolve between the two. Both are vehicles of communication, and in each instance, the formulas were skillfully calculated to package and sell not only the personality but the physical appearance of Ronald Reagan. The paramount consideration in building his image was to create credibility of the man to his audience, so that appearance became more important than substance or reality. As both actor and politician, the perfection of the pretense had to be persuasive beyond the shadow of a doubt to his ''pre-prepped'' audience.

Through years of practical experience, Reagan learned well the technique of playing to the camera in a completely natural way and was never intimidated by the lens. The camera appeared to transmit the essential Reagan, cool and relaxed, to film and tape with an ease of illusion. The major legacy of his acting career to his role as president was his unique ability to create the impression that his fantasy screen image — the all-American nice guy, firm in his convictions, yet amiable and decent — was actually the man himself.

His mastery of decisive, sincere, straightforward image projection was ideal for television, which is able to give the appearance of substance, breadth, and depth. Culminating in Reagan's celebrification of politics, television has become the postmodern portrait gallery in which issues are subordinated to images. Commercial television must sell products; this is done by showing the potential consumer appealing pictures that often have nothing to do with the product itself. Reagan's emergence on the political stage, straight from central casting, has changed the rules of the game of telepolitics, and the 1980s have become a watershed for all future presidents. In the post-McLuhan age of the visual image, the candidate's ability to come across on television has overshadowed substantive issues, so that the selling of the president has become interchangeable with that of soft drinks or soap. In each instance the product is frequently wrapped in the American flag. Simplification of language accompanies the glossy visuals so that memorized one-liners, buzzwords, tag lines, and slogans facilitate the shorter collective attention span of the audience.

Rooted in the mass-cultural capital of the United States, Reagan's recognition factor as a pre-sold public figure gave him an extraordinary political advantage when he began his career in public life. Feeling that he could never be overrehearsed, he achieved an aggressively attractive image with a cereal commercial down-home folksiness at the heart of an appealingly enthusiastic and convincingly forthright personality.

As the country's father figure, he became the ultimate consumer commodity, the telegenic leading man and the star of the show, with the presidency itself another form of show business. The political actor's made-for-television presidency had all the right stuff — the look, timing, gesture, and voice modulations — to make him one of the most popular presidents in a nation enchanted with celebrities. His voice was particularly effective — intimate and mellifluous, as though he were sharing his thoughts and ideas with a few trusted friends. The theatrical element in politics is certainly not new — powerful leaders from Julius Caesar through Napolean to deGaulle and Kennedy have been consummate showmen who have had the ability to make themselves larger than life and have established a credibility beyond what the facts could justify. Ronald Reagan, however, went one step further by irrevocably erasing all distinctions between theater and public life.

Throughout the past millenia, painters, sculptors, and graphic artists have always taken the portrait as one of their major themes. The portrayal of the human face as a unique phenomenon and a key to individual personality has enabled future generations to gain knowledge of and insight into past civilizations. Over the centuries, the art of portraiture has undergone far-reaching transformations. At the end of the eighteenth century, 200 years before the emergence of Ronald Reagan, the face and form of George Washington was preserved for future generations of Americans in visual representations. As the father of the country and its first president, Washington was painted in the grand manner by leading artists Gilbert Stuart, Charles Willson Peale, John Trumbull, and Rembrandt Peale; he was sculpted by Jean Antoine Houdon (from life) and Horatio Greenough (posthumously). Washington was painted from life by 28 artists from Edward Savage and William Dunlap to Joseph Wright and James Shaples, yet it is the image by Gilbert Stuart that dominates all others. Lithography made possible the wide distribution of Washington's image in his own time, and the printing of the dollar bill helped to preserve its currency. Forty years after Washington's death Greenough's heroic marble sculpture of him was installed in the Capitol rotunda. Greenough had based the figure, which is naked to the waist, on the statue of Zeus made by Phidias in the 5th century B.C. In 1851 Emanuel Leutze attempted to reconstruct American history with his aloof, godlike figure of the president in *Washington Crossing the Delaware*. The allegorical and cinematic qualities of this painting have inspired such diverse twentieth-century artists as Grant Wood, Larry Rivers, John Wesley, Robert Colescott, and Sante Graziani. Washington's symbolic role cannot be underestimated, nor can the impact his image has exerted on all future generations of American artists and the way in which they saw their leaders.

The advent of photography 150 years ago radically transformed portraiture, making it no longer a necessity for recording history or identifying individuals. The more recent pervasiveness of motion pictures and the omnipresent image on the television screen have brought about a reappraisal of portraiture as an artistic medium. With the dominance of photography and television, portraiture is no longer a major branch of painting, especially for recording and preserving the images of world leaders. Despite the popularity and supremacy of photography and television, a small minority of artists continued to create portraits. Beginning in the 1960s there was a resurgence of portraiture by a variety of serious professional artists whose major work lay outside the confinements of formal portraiture. This revival of interest in political portraiture reached its peak in the Reagan years, having been in a state of dormancy for over a century.

The major artists who took Washington as their subject in the late eighteenth century perpetuated the tradition into the nineteenth century, during which it briefly flourished before going into a long decline. Gilbert Stuart took the lead by painting Washington's successors in office: John Adams, Thomas Jefferson, James Madison, James Monroe, and John Quincy Adams. John Trumbull, on the other hand, only painted two presidents, John Adams and Thomas Jefferson, after his portraits of Washington, and worked in New York and London, rather than compete with Stuart in Boston. John Vanderlyn was another important presidential portraitist; besides his posthumous portrait of Washington, he had painted James Madison, James Monroe, Andrew Jackson, and Zachary Taylor. Thomas Sully, who had painted Queen Victoria, also did portraits of John Quincy Adams, Andrew Jackson, James Monroe, and Thomas Jefferson. Among the other noted American artists who occasionally executed presidential portraits were John Singleton Copley (John Adams), Mather Brown (John Adams and Thomas Jefferson), Charles Wesley Jarvis (Thomas Jefferson), Charles Bird King (James Monroe), George Caleb Bingham (John Quincy Adams), Ralph E. W. Earl (Andrew Jackson), Henry Inman (Martin Van Buren), and Eastman Johnson (John Quincy Adams, Grover Cleveland, and Benjamin Harrison). The most prolific painter of American presidents in the nineteenth century, however, was George Peter Alexander Healy, who painted portraits of Presidents Jackson, Van Buren, Tyler, Polk, Fillmore, Pierce, Buchanan, Lincoln, Grant, and Arthur. Healy was America's first international portraitist and made the first of his 34 Atlantic crossings in 1834. French King Louis Philippe commissioned him to paint portraits of American presidents and other leaders in 1842.

The greatest American portraitist of the nineteenth century, Thomas Eakins, unfortunately never painted a president. Despite one last gasp of American grand-style portraiture in the latter part of the last century by John Singer Sargent, William Merritt Chase, and James Abbott McNeill Whistler, there were few really outstanding or highly original depictions of presidents from the mid-nineteenth through the mid-twentieth century.

The presidency of John Fitzgerald Kennedy coincided with the emergence in the early 1960s of the Pop Art movement and the return to figurative art after a period in which abstraction had been dominant. Kennedy, the second youngest president in our history, was the most glamorous and physically attractive man in this century to occupy the White House when he took office. It should come as no surprise then, that after Reagan, the Kennedy image was the most pervasive and popular presidential subject for leading twentieth-century artists. The majority of the Kennedy portraits, however, were executed after his untimely assassination,

by such artists as Robert Rauschenberg, Jasper Johns, Claes Oldenburg, James Rosenquist, and Andy Warhol. Rauschenberg's works, especially in the 1960s and 1970s, abounded with the faces of political leaders: President Dwight D. Eisenhower, Martin Luther King, Jr., Robert Kennedy, Joseph Stalin, Queen Elizabeth, Malcolm X, Senator Jacob Javits, and George Wallace. In addition to the Americans, artists from abroad, such as Richard Hamilton, Martial Raysse, and Fujio Nuva, found magic in the Kennedy image. Many official portraits of Kennedy, mostly on commission, were also done by Elaine de Kooning, Rene Bouche, Pietro Annigoni, Boris Chaliapin, and William Franklin Draper. Kennedy is well-remembered through the diversity of these painted images, yet a remarkable photographic legacy of this president by such talented photographers as Arnold Newman, Mark Shaw, Elliott Erwitt, Philippe Halsman, Garry Winogrand, Alfred Eisenstaedt, Yousuf Karsh, and Arthur Rothstein also lives on.

Like all presidents since John Quincy Adams, who was the first to have his likeness recorded on an extant daguerreotype in 1843, Kennedy and Reagan have been the subject of a myriad of photographic images. The arrival of photography around 1840 coincided with the transition from ruling aristocratic elite to a more populist government, personified by President Andrew Jackson. The camera was the ideal medium for this transition for, unlike painting, photography was the great equalizer. James K. Polk was the first president to be photographed in the White House. The great photographer Mathew Brady, who had an extraordinary sense of the importance of documenting history, not only left posterity a remarkable visual record of the Civil War, but also photographed numerous presidents including John Quincy Adams, Andrew Jackson, Martin Van Buren, James K. Polk, Zachary Taylor, Millard Fillmore, James Buchanan, Abraham Lincoln, and Ulysses S. Grant. Among numerous excellent examples of nineteenth-century photographic portraits of presidents, a sampling might include Southworth & Hawes' Franklin Pierce, Samuel F. B. Morse's Andrew Jackson, Alexander Gardner's Abraham Lincoln, and Timothy O'Sullivan's Ulysses S. Grant. In addition, two presidential portraits — Zachary Taylor and Millard Fillmore — have been attributed to Southworth & Hawes.

As the sheer volume of photographs increased with each administration in the twentieth century, fewer painters and sculptors regarded the image of the president as serious subject matter for their work. Theodore Roosevelt, the first president to complete his elected terms of office in this century, would have made a marvelous subject for a major painter working in the grand style; instead, his likeness was preserved by three great photographic masters: Edward S. Curtis, Alvin Langdon Coburn, and Edward Steichen. Although no leading American artists painted presidential portraits in the late nineteenth or early twentieth century, two prominent European artists did accomplish this. The Swedish artist Anders Zorn painted Grover Cleveland two years after he completed his second term in office, and also did a portrait of William Howard Taft. Taft was also the subject of a portrait in oil by the Spanish painter Joaquin Sarolla and a photographic work by Edward Steichen. The most enduring images of Calvin Coolidge were done by photographers Nickolas Muray and Doris Ulmann. Herbert Hoover was painted by Edmund Charles Tarbell, who had previously done a portrait of Woodrow Wilson. However, Hoover's most significant portraits remain the photographs by Edward Steichen, Imogen Cunningham, and Nickolas Muray.

Franklin D. Roosevelt, for all his popularity and support of artists in the W.P.A., was never the subject of mainstream American painters, although two leading sculptors, Reuben Nakian and Jo Davidson, did three-dimensional bust portraits of him. Davidson also executed competent likenesses of Presidents Wilson, Hoover, and Eisenhower. Roosevelt's enduring visual impression, however, is in his photographic heritage by such masters as Edward Steichen, Erich Salomon, Margaret Bourke-White, Nickolas Muray, Yousuf Karsh, Arthur Rothstein, Alfred Eisenstaedt, Thomas D. McAvoy, and Hansel Mieth.

In a humorous color lithograph by Ben Shahn entitled *A Good Man Is Hard To Find,* Harry S Truman is shown playing an upright piano, with his Republican opponent Thomas E. Dewey perched on top. The work is based on a photograph by Charles Cort in which Truman is playing the piano with actress Lauren Bacall reclining over it. Shahn was one of the leading American artists working during the Truman administration, and it is ironic that his one memorable presidential work was based on a photograph. One of the most famous photographs of an American president in the twentieth century is the 1948 image by Al Muto of a triumphantly grinning Truman holding up a copy of the *Chicago Daily Tribune* with the headline, ''Dewey Defeats Truman.'' Besides these provocative photojournalistic images by Cort and Muto, Truman was photographed by Arnold Newman, Horst, Gjon Mili, Eliot Elisofon, Arthur Rothstein, Alfred Eisenstaedt, Yousuf Karsh, Mark Kauffman, and Katherine Young.

America's best-known illustrator, Norman Rockwell, did commissioned paintings of several presidents, including Eisenhower, Johnson and Nixon, as well as one of Reagan when he was governor of California. Dwight D. Eisenhower, like Franklin D. Roosevelt before him, did not evoke much interest from American painters. Eisenhower's silkscreened double image does, however, appear in Robert Rauschenberg's *Factum I and II* of 1957. Rauschenberg lifted Eisenhower's picture from a newspaper photograph and made it a part of his overall composition. Many leading photographers have recorded Eisenhower's features, such as Richard Avedon, Cecil Beaton, Eve Arnold, Yousuf Karsh, David Douglas Duncan, Alfred Eisenstaedt, Arnold Newman, Arthur Rothstein, James Whitmore, and Francis Miller.

After Reagan and Kennedy, Lyndon B. Johnson probably captured the imagination of more of this century's artists than any other president. While in office, he did much to support the arts, and was the subject of a large wooden sculpture by Marisol, and was painted by Larry Rivers and Peter Hurd, as well as Pietro Annigoni. He was photographed by such now-familiar names as Arnold Newman, Arthur Rothstein, Alfred Eisenstaedt, and Ken Heyman. In contrast to Johnson, Richard M. Nixon elicited scant scrutiny from artists, but attracted the attention of an unprecedented number of mainstream twentieth-century photographers, including Robert Frank, Jane Bown, Philippe Halsman, Eve Arnold, Garry Winogrand, Arnold Newman, Alfred Eisenstaedt, Tony Spina, Katherine Young, Arthur Rothstein, Elliott Erwitt, and David Douglas Duncan.

Reagan's two immediate predecessors in the oval office were also of more interest to photographers than they were to painters or sculptors. Gerald R. Ford was captured by the lens of Richard Avedon, David Kennerly, Alfred Eisenstaedt, and Arthur Rothstein.

Although Andy Warhol and James B. Wyeth painted portraits of Jimmy Carter, his image was more forcibly rendered by three discerning photographers: Ansel Adams, Richard Avedon, and Arthur Rothstein.

In terms of Reagan's own photographic images, he had, of course, been the subject of Hollywood's greatest still photographers for several decades. Two photographers humorously captured Reagan's image before he became president. Weegee's work from the mid-1960s is a distorted-mirror photograph of him with the inscription, ''For President Gov. Reagan.'' In the ''Suburbia'' series of photographs by Bill Owens from 1972, Reagan appears on the screen of a television set. He is dressed in full military costume, and the TV set is situated in the center of a suburban living room next to a huge Christmas tree and elaborately wrapped gifts. In addition, two outstanding photographers a decade apart, made strong images of Reagan. In the mid-1970s Richard Avedon photographed a half-length portrait of a stern and serious Reagan dressed in a business suit with arms rigidly at his sides and looking directly at the viewer. Although the photograph by Michael Evans from the mid-1980s presents the president in similar dress and pose, Evans' Reagan looks a decade younger than he had in the Avedon photo. The Evans image presents Reagan as a vigorously buoyant and happy man, clasping his hands in front of him in a gesture of confidence and authority.

Ronald Reagan caught the pulse of serious American artists as no other president has done since the early nineteenth century. In addition to depicting Reagan's physical features, all of the artists who dealt with him were acutely aware of his relationship to the media, especially television. Whether explicitly or implicitly, the media is a constant and recurring theme in all of the Reagan works. Ironically, despite his long career as an actor in motion pictures, few artists make direct reference to that part of his past. Andy Warhol, who had previously painted portraits of Kennedy, Nixon and Carter, makes an indirect allusion to Reagan's career in pictures in *Van Heusen (Ronald Reagan)*. His silkscreen paintings utilize a photograph of an old shirt ad, which was originally part of a promotional campaign for Reagan's 1953 film, *Law and Order*. The work is a sly comment on his "Teflon" Presidency, as the ad copy states: "Won't wrinkle ever." Warhol painted the screen in a deliberately careless way so that the image is distorted and much more brightly colored than the original. In this latter-day recycling of Charles Dana Gibson's Arrow Collar man, Reagan is again the pin-up poster man in which surface is essence.

Reagan the actor is implicit in many of the works when artists depict him in various guises or roles that reverberate back to his acting career on a subliminal level. In these subtle, allegorical paintings and sculptures, Reagan is seen in a dazzling repertoire of roles: a mythological Greek centaur (Komar & Melamid), an American eagle promoting jelly beans (Jimmy Ernst), a tortoise (Tim Rollins & K.O.S.), a bird (Prigov), Dracula (Glier), George III (Sandlin), Rocky Balboa (Hofmekler), Charlie Chaplin (Hofmekler), a television set (Arneson), a Molotov cocktail (Wojarnowicz), a cowboy (Castrucci), a wrestler (Castrucci), a hunter (Sandlin), a woman (Saul), a faceless man (Kosalapov), a saint (Clarke), a human jail (Van Dalen), a ventriloquist (Cole), a man with no lips (Conal), a scientific wizard (Haney), Repo Man (Kearns), Uncle Sam (Larson), and the ultimate corporate man (McFadden). Thus, many of the artists view Reagan as a political chameleon, a quick-change artist whose ease at changing costumes for different roles

is paralleled by his ability to change his political skin.

The symbolic content in these works is rich and multilayered. His role in *Bedtime for Bonzo* was that of a psychology professor who sets out to prove the ascendancy of nurture over nature by raising a chimp in his own house. His close identification with the role may have prompted artists to depict Reagan himself as an animal, in a reversal of roles. Rollins & K.O.S. present the face of Reagan on a turtle, with the book pages of George Orwell's *Animal Farm* serving as background. Komar & Melamid's *Portrait of Ronald Reagan as a Centaur* parallels ancient Greek mythology, which has the power to lift mortal men to Olympus, with the fantasy machine of Hollywood film that transforms a midwestern sportscaster into a venerated movie star and then into president. The massive, overdeveloped musculature of the centaur echoes the macho, beefcake pin-ups for which Reagan had posed in Hollywood. The heroic proportions of the mythological beast, with emphasis on physical strength, virility, and potency, implies amorous exploits and erotic stamina and thereby recalls Reagan's years as a "Hollywood bachelor."

For the public, movie stars resembled Greek heroes or gods with their romances, foibles, and personal tragedies magnified by the press and made into instant mythology. Just as the love lives of the gods were chronicled in ancient mythology, the Hollywood scribes recorded an endless parade of Reagan's epic romantic attachments prior to his second marriage, visually and verbally detailing his relationships with a number of actresses including Ruth Roman, Ann Southern, Doris Day, Shelly Winters, Patricia Neal, Piper Laurie, Monica Lewis, Adele Mara, Adele Jergens, Penny Edwards, Kay Stewart, Myrna Dell, Betty Underwood, Dorothy Shay, Doris Lilly, Shirley Ballard, and Cookie Gordon.

Many film and television roles required Reagan to ride horses, and off-camera he has long been associated with horses, both as a breeder and an accomplished rider. Throughout his presidency, he was repeatedly photographed with pet dogs and other animals, so it is not surprising that animals symbolically appear with him in many of the artists' works: a horse (Haney), a dog (Sandlin), birds (Grooms and Cole), cows (Kosalapov), pigs (Goodman and Glier), and even a bee (Huffaker).

Many other symbols, most of them with violent associations, further echo Reagan's film and television roles. The perpetual presence of guns in *Death Valley Days* and in such films as *Sergeant Murphy, Secret Service of the Air, Code of the Secret Service, Smashing the Money Ring, Murder in the Air, Santa Fe Trail, The Bad Man, International Squadron, Desperate Journey, Storm Warning, The Last Outpost, Hong Kong, Tropic Zone, Law and Order, Prisoner of War, Cattle Queen of Montana, Tennessee's Partner,* and *The Killers* attest to gun collector Reagan's established identification with them. The gun is the most often recurring and profoundly male icon in film, and is to be found, somewhat benignly, in Sandlin's and Castrucci's paintings with Reagan as hunter and cowboy, respectively, but more menacingly in Cole's and Clarke's works. The deplorable effect of guns in American society is dealt with in both Minter's and Kearns' works. Other symbols of violence include a knife and stick of dynamite (Marcus), a Molotov cocktail and skulls (Wojnarowicz), boxing gloves (Hofmekler), steel helmets and gas masks (Glier), long-range missiles (Haney, Grooms, Larson, Jaar, and Haacke), and blood (Saul and Glier).

In works by Saul and Glier, blood is equated with money, as it is in *Repo Man* by Kearns. Glier's *Give Blood* criticizes Reagan's refusal of adequate funding for the homeless, the elderly, children, and the environment in favor of his increase in military spending. With fangs bared, a giant head of Reagan in the center of the black and white composition looms out, surrounded by giant lettering spelling out the words "give blood." In Saul's *Ronald Reagan #5 (Tits),* the fang-bearing face of Reagan is placed on a female form with bloody mammary glands labeled "domestic" and "foreign." In public speeches, Reagan habitually made reference to himself as bleeding, such as his self-description as once having been "a hemophiliac liberal — I bled for 'causes,' " or "I bled real blood for the unemployed." His choice of language often included such descriptions as "cutting and slashing" of the "hemorrhaging budgets."

The theme of the federal deficit appears in Saul's "Lunch" series, in which Reagan is eating a "money sandwich" consisting of five-dollar bills on white bread. Fighting the deficit is humorously shown in Hofmekler's *Ronny II,* with an out-of-shape president in boxing trunks and official seal with gloves inscribed "federal reserve" in a take-off on Sylvester Stallone's *Rocky* movies. Reagan's cutting of federal programs for students, minorities, the elderly, small business, day care, cities, Haitians, and the ERA is symbolically depicted in Van Dalen's *Reagan's Prison,* in which the prison consists of a large wooden head of Reagan, with barred windows indicating each underfunded program, a black metal tongue with a white, unlit votive candle protruding from the open mouth, and stenciled lettering stating "The Crime Show — ABC No Rio."

Haackes' *Reaganomics* is a reflection of the President's 23-year-old son in a Manhattan unemployment line in 1982 and contains the wording: "Yes my son collects unemployment, too!"

REAGANOMICS." The tax-exempt donations to refurbish the Reagans' living quarters in the White House and the First Lady's wardrobe were the targets of Haackes' *The Safety Net*, in which another large photograph of Reagan is shown with the words: "You want some advice? We got $800,000 to fix up our place, all tax-exempt. And many of Nancy's designer clothes are donated. Try charity!" The pervasive role of mammonish greed in the media is a theme of Minter's *Reagan Wallpaper*, in which repeated television screens with a freeze frame of the President being shot are juxtaposed with stenciled details of George Washington's engraved likeness from the one dollar bill. In numerous lucrative films, Reagan was either sick, injured, or dying: *Knute Rockne — All American, The Bad Man, Kings Row, Stallion Road, Night Unto Night,* and *The Winning Team.*

Patriotic symbols also abound, with the American eagle and flag emblazoned on Grooms' pull-toy, and both the Statue of Liberty and the American flag in the form of Reagan's tie in Marcus' works. Reagan is shown extinguishing the torch of freedom on Lady Liberty atop a huge birthday cake covered with a map of the world in a painting entitled *Blowing It*. One of the President's more benign symbols, the jar of jelly beans, is included in the works of Arneson and Ernst. The jelly beans derive from the Reagans' mutual decision to give up smoking after the death of their friend Robert Taylor from lung cancer in 1968 and their motto: "reach for the jelly bean instead of a smoke." Multiple symbols, in the form of company logos, form the head of McFadden's portrait of Reagan in which his very identity merges with the Fortune 500 corporations. The implication is that Reagan was a creation of America's corporate power structure and that he embodies their interests above all else.

Many of the works are concerned with the Reagan administration's foreign policy, especially toward the Soviet Union and Nicaragua. In Burson's *Warhead IV,* Reagan's facial features literally merge with those of Mikhail Gorbachev in a computer-generated photo composite, while Jaar juxtaposes large color photographs of the faces of the two world leaders in a light box, which also contains a wheat field and airborne missiles. Larson places Gorbachev, dressed as a Russian soldier, and Reagan, dressed as Uncle Sam, facing each other with missiles poised on a parallel bar with a gear that alternately raises and lowers their positions. The balance of power is also the theme of Grooms' *Nuclear Nuts* in which the two leaders are shaking hands while standing on a horizontally positioned missile with a pull-toy detonator deciding which one has the leverage at any given time.

In Haney's *Wizard of Never, Never Land,* Reagan is posed pondering the complicated machinery of "Star Wars" laser technology while a missile is being launched over his head. Similarly, the dangerous, expensive, and unworkable aspects of "Star Wars" are underscored in Haacke's *We Bring Good Things to Life*. The title is a reference to General Electric, the nation's fourth largest military contractor, for which Reagan served as a television actor and spokesman in the 1950s and 1960s. An equally chilling commentary on Reagan's attempts to promote a nuclear arms build-up with speeches in Germany is presented in Haacke's *Oelgemaelde, Hommage à Marcel Broodthaers*. Haacke's two-part work consists of an imperial portrait of Reagan facing a large photographic blow-up of a protest demonstration. Cold war politics, espionage, duplicity, and the ticking away of a time bomb are among the issues raised in Kearns' *Repo Man*. Leslie's official-looking double portrait of 1984, done on commission for Time, Inc., presents a stately and serious President back to back with his antagonist, Soviet President Yuri Andropov.

Reagan's Latin American foreign policy is dealt with in works by Cole and Clarke. *Postcard from Nicaragua* by Cole is critical of the administration's role in Nicaragua, particularly covert operations, and presents a collage of symbols of oppression. In one small element of the collage, Reagan appears in a photograph next to a picture of an ancient red jaguar with the inscription: "The red jaguar vs. the ventriloquist." Clarke is less specific in his painting *Fledgling Democracy*, which depicts a scene of fascist political terrorism that could be taking place in El Salvador, Nicaragua, or any Latin American Third World country. Reagan stands outside the Spanish-style house conferring with his aides Meese and Abrams, while inside a family is being terrorized by guerrilla soldiers. In Clarke's *Ronald Reagan*, the tuxedo-clad President stands holding a red book while his advisers flutter around his head, whispering advice into his ear. Reagan holds center stage in the central gold-leaf panel, surrounded by smaller panels in the manner of an Italian Renaissance altarpiece.

In Sivilli's *The Cancelling Out of Icons,* Reagan's face floats in and out of the lithograph while other faces from distant cultures overlap and are superimposed on his. The relativity of leaders, icons, and idols is also the theme of Kosalapov's *Hero, Leader, God,* which juxtaposes three gigantic heads against a blue sky: hero (the Apollo Belvedere), leader (a faceless Reagan), and god (Spiderman). Kosalapov has obliterated Reagan's features, reducing him to a mindless product of the media that is capable of elevating a comic-book character to the status of god, interchangeable with a mythological hero or with the President himself.

Both Brown and Verona painted double portraits of Nancy and Ronald together. Veroha's beatific cut-out couple smile out of a shaped canvas photo opportunity. In Brown's version, the Presidential couple's idealized smiling features appear in the clouds above a stylized suburban American neighborhood. At first glance they seem to be glorified, but the clouds are dark and look polluted, and the couple is placed above the ordinary concern of ordinary people. Robbie Conal, working from newspaper photographs, has painted a black and white image of Nancy Reagan as

one of four portraits in "Women with Teeth"; the other three portraits are of Margaret Thatcher, Jean Kirkpatrick, and Joan Rivers. A companion work to this quartet is "Men with No Lips," with portraits of Ronald Reagan, Donald Regan, Caspar Weinberger, and James A. Baker III. Conal's single portrait/poster of Reagan is entitled "Contra Diction." Sandlin's twin portraits, *President Ronald Reagan as Charles III in Hunting Dress after Goya* and *First Lady Nancy Reagan as the Marquesa De Pontejos after Goya,* portray them both as aristocrats who associate with wealthy right-wingers.

Dreiblatt's sketch of Nancy in red, taken from a photograph, places her detached head in an ambiguous scene with two grieving nuns rendered in blue pencil. Brezinski's bold woodcut of Nancy in a red dress in an otherwise black and white composition recalls German Expressionism. Castrucci's *I Love You Nancy Show* shows a smiling President with Nancy on his mind against a raw, graffiti-like background.

Several artists have successfully drawn on past movements and styles to make an ironic comment on the 1980s. Kosalapov's and Komar & Melamid's updated reinterpretations of classical mythology present Reagan in the light of the past. Clarke has based his composition for *Fledgling Democracy* on Piero della Francesca's *The Flagellation of Christ*, condensing and reversing the three conferring figures to the left side of the picture. *Ronald*

Reagan, also by Clarke, is an elaborate, compartmentalized composition suggested by Sienese painter Simone Martini's *The Blessed Agostino Novello.* Sandlin has based his twin portraits of the Reagans on eighteenth-century paintings by Francisco Goya, using the same stance and composition, but modernizing their costumes. Twentieth-century masters also inspired several of the painters. Warhol owes a debt to Marcel Duchamp in his use of the commercial advertisement. Kosalapov based his Reagan head on the pre-1920s mannequin heads of Giorgio de Chirico. The series of painted bottles from the 1940s and 1950s by René Magritte were the inspirations for Wojnarowicz's Molotov cocktail "Night Train" bottle with gold skulls entitled *Variation on Magritte's Bottle.*

The majority of artists discreetly posed Reagan in the official dress of a business suit and tie: Brown, Burson, Castrucci, Clarke, Cole, Conal, Grooms, Haacke, Haney, Huffaker, Jaar, Kearns, Kosalapov, Leslie, Marcus, McKay, Minter, Saul, Sivilli, Smith, and Verona. Reagan's world has become a global stage, and he is pictured as a man of action who is continuously on the move, shaking hands with Gorbachev (Grooms), campaigning in Iowa with his hand on a pig (Goodman), marveling over "Star Wars" technology (Haney), deliberating with aides (Clarke), eating money sandwiches and abortion material (Saul), blowing out liberty's candle (Marcus), waving a red banner (Komar & Melamid), and waving from a television set (Arneson).

Reagan's masterful stagecraft and complete identification with the medium of television are given the ultimate statement in the two sculptures by Arneson, *Ronny Portable* in bronze and *Ronny (26" Model)* in ceramic. Arneson, who earlier had juxtaposed George Washington with the Mona Lisa, goes beyond symbolism to living personification in which Reagan's identity is completely merged with the television set. Inscriptions on the back of the set read: "Caution: Do not expose this appliance to thought or reason," and "Warning: Service by modern Hollywood screen fantasies only." Minter has depicted Reagan at the moment of John Hinckley's assassination attempt on multiple TV screens receding into space in *Reagan Wallpaper.* The computer drawings of Gregg Smith capture the multiple distortions of a basic TV image, but his painting shows the smiling media president in a very upbeat image. Huffaker's humorous portrait of Reagan, *Bzzzt!,* is also a smiling face of the president with an "MX bee" going in one ear and out the other.

Goodman places the made-for-television president on an urban stage in *A Day in the City,* but he is out of place and unconnected to the crowds of animated people, concentrating instead on a black pig, which is a symbol of gluttony. Wit McKay's computer acrylic images of Reagan profoundly comment on his telegenic persona, The Great Communicator. The pictures are distorted and out of focus like TV images one might catch out of the corner of one's eye, not really looking at the screen. Recalling the stylization of Francis Bacon, McKay has captured the flickering TV image which has passed in and out of our lives and in and out of time over the years.

As with all durable Hollywood movie stars, the Reagan image underwent subtle modifications to conform with certain styles and trends of each decade in which he was before the cameras. Making his first major career shift in the late 1930s from radio sports announcer to actor in feature films, Reagan changed in a more pronounced way than when he moved from motion pictures into television. The future president began his career in television as an actor in the early 1950s and then became announcer, host, commercial spokesman, and, finally, political spokesman. These transitions were seamless and the alterations almost imperceptible. The mechanics of this image-building, forged in Hollywood, streamlined in Sacramento, and transferred, with slight modifications, to the highest office in the land, are singularly phenomenal.

Ronald Reagan's essential Hollywood image was repackaged and fine-tuned to meet Washington specifications; but even though he was given the power look personifying leadership, determination, firmness, and self-esteem, what the American electorate received in 1980 and 1984 was fundamental Hollywood fantasy. Although in his role as president, Reagan became more patriarchal, confident, and authoritarian, his basic Hollywood image was left intact: the clean-cut, all-American who was outgoing, pleasant, personable, enthusiastic, athletic, bland, wholesome, patriotic, trustworthy, loyal, brave, true blue, self-effacing, and puppy dog friendly. Warner Brothers had molded him in the innocently average, benignly normal American cast alongside the likes of Gary Cooper, Joel McCrea, Randolph Scott, and Henry Fonda. These archetypal American actors represented the decent common man, the ordinary guy next door whose rugged but responsible individualism was unambiguous and incorruptible. He was a dutiful, democratic man of principle, courage, stoicism, and integrity in the best American tradition.

The fresh, boyish qualities associated with the young Reagan were indistinguishable from those of scores of young men from a seemingly interchangeable gene pool who were storming the studio gates in the late 1930s. He bore similarities to the dreamily dewy and antiseptically clean-cut looks of other starlads such as Lew Ayres, Richard Arlen, Charles ''Buddy'' Rogers, John Boles, Franchot Tone, and Robert Young. The formula image, which worked very effectively for James Stewart, George Murphy, and Fred MacMurray, was that of an upbeat ''Mr. Norm'' with a sunny bonhomie, and an it's-great-to-be-alive manner. A genial, smooth graciousness gave the assurance that this type of man would always be respectful to his elders and betters, and could be counted on to do the predictably right thing. In addition, he possessed a youthful naive innocence and moral purity which accounted for his breezy optimism and sweetness-and-light disposition. His good-hearted virtues were constantly highlighted and reinforced in that Hollywood plot conventions invariably pitted him against adversaries of lesser mettle.

The careful grooming by Warner Brothers emphasized Reagan's clean, bright attributes and made him ideal for light, romantic leading man roles; but these same attributes were not what the top flight directors were looking for when casting the heavy dramatic parts in their prestigious pictures. As a result, the range of Reagan's roles was restricted to playing in the standard programmers that Hollywood indiscriminately turned out by the hundreds. The advantages of being under contract to Warner Brothers, however, were considerable: studio grooming and an apprenticeship that included a myth-support system of publicity and the assurance of production and cast quality. Reagan worked repeatedly with the studio's house directors, producers, and other stars to solidify a strong hold on the collective mythic imagination of the audience. The slow, steady accumulation of his roles over a period of many years etched his admirable image deeply into the soul of the American public. Increasingly, he fulfilled the role of a strong, steady, solid father figure whose patriarchal attributes were those of the reliable provider and protector.

Throughout his long career, Reagan was confined to the lower echelon of Hollywood actors. This was a situation he seemed to accept cheerfully, but it must have been frustrating at times, since, on several occasions, he came very close to breaking into the superstar bracket, most notably in *Knute Rockne - All American, Kings Row,* and *The Hasty Heart.* The majority of scripts assigned to him by Warner Brothers, however, were lightweight, transparent, and unchallenging, but ironically, they did not interfere much with his own statement of who he was. Despite the array of characters and vocations which he assumed in his roles, he never wavered from being typecast basically as himself, and he maintained the ability to inhabit his own identity to the fullest. Although these mediocre roles were romantic, sentimental, and by no means intellectually challenging, Reagan could be counted on to give a performance that was sincere, simple, straightforward and direct, untainted by affectation, and rarely ambivalent.

Cast as the dumb, gee-whiz, small-town kid with little inner conflict, his innocence was indistinguishable from ignorance, which was equated with being "natural." In many of these parts, he was the easily revved-up hick or hayseed who was not too educationally advanced. Occasionally this yokel role was taken to the brink of mental infantilism. In other parts in which he attempted to be elegant and dapper, he was less successful. He was programmed to represent the average American, often from the Midwest, slightly shy, neither smarter nor dumber than the everyman in the audience, who learned to identify with Reagan's handsome face and body. Simultaneously, this image was calculated to cause women to buy the myth of romantic possibility and to indulge in their erotic fantasies.

As a competent, second-string journeyman actor in the Warner Brothers stable, he ground out 30 films during his first five years at the studio. Although he began playing the lead role in "B" films *(Love Is on the Air)* and supporting roles in "A" films *(Dark Victory),* the majority of his Hollywood parts were not in "B" films per se. His entertaining but routine films at Warner Brothers were closer to "A−" or "B+," and the true "B" films in which he did appear occurred either very early or very late in his career. Summing up his early roles, Reagan refers to himself as "the Errol Flynn of the Bs." During the 1930s and 1940s, when he made the majority of his films, it was not uncommon for "A" films to be photographed in black and white. Of Reagan's 53 films, only ten were shot in color. Shorter feature films of an hour or less were, for the most part, in the category of "B" films. The length of Reagan's films ranged from 55 minutes for *Murder in the Air* to 130 minutes for *Kings Row.* The latter film was so popular that it was made into a television series in 1955, as one of three rotating elements of *Warner Brothers Presents.* Reagan's role of Drake McHugh was played in the series by Robert Horton.

It is difficult to break down the individual components of Reagan's Hollywood image, for the look, the character, and the role were inseparable. An entire industry of Hollywood masterminds was engaged in the manufacture and exploitation of emerging star images. These experts labored to smooth all rough edges and to enhance the physical beauty and erotic appeal of young contract players. Their image-building fabrication required each studio to have a veritable army of makeup artists, hairdressers, trainers, and wardrobe personnel who were prepared to go to work on the new faces and bodies. They dyed and transplanted hair, capped teeth, padded over inadequacies, squeezed torsos into girdles, elevated shoes, dressed and undressed, fought for flattering camera angles, and lifted and cosmetically made over faces.

In 1937, they applied their skill and alchemy to re-creating Ronald Reagan in Hollywood's image, concocting a new man for the world to see. Their image-building went beyond the physical make-over to include promotional and marketing strategies to sell their product to the public. In print, the actor's physical and mental virtues were extolled, and his sex appeal described in great detail.

Shortly after his arrival in Hollywood in 1937, Reagan was sent by Warner Brothers to the House of Westmore where he was turned over to Perc Westmore. Westmore cut and reshaped his heavy thatch of hair, moving the part from the middle of his head to the left side. Shortly thereafter Westmore decided that the part in Reagan's hair looked better on the right side, where it remained for 50 years. He was also given a large pompadour, or pouf, which seemed to increase in size over the years, with the hair on the sides and back of his head slicked into place. During his second year in Hollywood, the studio felt that his dark hair looked too Latin or Mediterranean on black and white film, so they lightened it to an auburn color to reinforce his all-American look.

Although the former sports announcer lacked a commanding presence and was rather stiff, awkward, and complacent, the studio worked hard to supply him with more color, passion, and warmth, bringing out what individuality he possessed. In Hollywood terms, he had the raw material with which the studio wizards could work: a large, well-shaped head in proportion to his torso; dark, thick hair; eyes wide apart and large in proportion to his face; high flung eyebrows; high forehead; straight, slender nose; square jaw; chiseled chin; slightly off-center smile; small ears; and slender but muscular build.

Since Reagan wore eyeglasses to correct nearsightedness, the studio supplied him with contact lenses. The years of wearing heavy glasses had created a deep crevice across the bridge of his nose, but this was corrected by an application of darker makeup and by creating imitation dimples and deeper laugh lines. Cinematographers quickly learned not to photograph Reagan full face in close-ups, as one eye had a tendency to turn slightly to the side at times. With a little help from the studio, the young star became well-groomed, clean shaven, and ramrod straight in posture. He had even learned how to lift his left eyebrow independently of the right. One of his greatest physical assets was his smile, which suggested that of a boy caught with his hand in the cookie jar, and most of his early roles required him to flash that famous grin consistently.

During his early years at Warner Brothers, the publicity department created an image of Reagan as a smooth, beach boy type and frequently had him passively pose for photographs shirtless or in swimsuits, often surrounded by a bevy of admiring bathing beauties. These semi-nude male pin-ups usually showed him well-tanned by the California sun, enjoying a variety of leisure activities. The frozen poses were designed to display the aesthetic male ideal — a well-developed muscularity which, especially in the 1940s and 1950s, functioned as a non-verbal symbol of gender dominance. Compared to heavy-duty 1980s screen idols Arnold Schwarzenegger and Sylvester Stallone, who have reigned supreme throughout Reagan's own administration, his muscular development seems rather modest. In the present decade, Hollywood male stars are measured more in terms of the size of their muscles than in terms of more conventional standards such as looks, charm, or acting ability. The 1980s body-builder-star type, with his overdeveloped, rippling musculature emphasizing bulk and massiveness, was not considered to be desirable, much less marketable, in the Hollywood of the 1940s. The standard of male glamour, seduction, and sex appeal was a less monumental physique; but it was muscularity, nevertheless, that was the body quality most promoted in Hollywood, and thus the key to appraising an actor's body.

Reagan typified the image of virile and robust physical fitness with a slender, muscular, and symmetrical physique. His body, at 180 pounds and six feet, one inch in height, with a 41-inch chest and a 32-inch waist, was considered to be the ideal in 1940. He had achieved this consummate perfection through years of swimming and football, and by breathing the clean air of the Midwest. In one promotional photo opportunity, Warner Brothers publicists sent him to the campus of the University of Southern California where they had him pose in white shorts for a sculpture class. The "news release" sent out with the photograph to daily papers announced that he had been chosen by the Fine Arts Department at U.S.C. as the male with the most perfect body. The studio created a twentieth-century Adonis for the mainstream popular culture. This not only kept fan mail pouring in to Warner Brothers, but also provided specific iconography for the adulatory fantasies of pubescent America.

Reagan's early physique photographs conformed to a systematic standardization of pose-repertory and contained an erotic subtext. The photographers went to much effort to invest these images with a quality of vacuous innocence and passive languor which communicated a casual availability. In these photographs, Reagan was being offered as an erotic spectacle within a context of passivity. In many of the poses, he does not look at the viewer, but usually gazes off or upward. When he does stare directly at the viewer, it is as if he is looking right through space to a place beyond the spectator. However passive and relaxed his poses, he invariably tightens and tautens his body, emphasizing his musculature by causing specific muscles to stand out, thus presenting an image of imminent activity and the body's potential for action.

These photographs were, of course, a male counterpart to the thriving cheesecake industry in mid-twentieth-century America. The male pin-ups were subject to more stigmatization than the female ones because undraped masculinity, especially presented in passive poses, went against the American grain. Society encouraged and expected women to display their bodies as beautiful objects, while the same behavior was traditionally frowned upon in men. For his studio, Reagan's body was very important for his image as an actor. Although these sessions tended to bolster an actor's vanity and exhibitionistic impulses, he had no choice in the matter of his availability for publicity photos, with or without clothes. It was a part of his contractual obligation to the studio; he would have risked suspension if he had refused to pose.

Errol Flynn received a similar bare-chested build-up by Warner Brothers, but from the onset, his image was less lethargic than Reagan's. The powers-that-be successfully turned Flynn into a vitally active, swashbuckling he-man and ultimately into a superstar in the romantic tradition of Douglas Fairbanks, Sr., Rudolph Valentino, George O'Brien, and Johnny Weissmuller. Each Hollywood studio was busily grooming and promoting its own stable of muscular male stars. The competitiveness among these magnificent specimens was intense and often ruthless, and Reagan had plenty of beefcake competition from such actors as Alan Ladd, Victor Mature, Sterling Hayden, Robert Stack, Cornel Wilde, John Payne, Burt Lancaster, Kirk Douglas, Guy Madison, and many others. Success in the industry could be bolstered by the size of an actor's muscles and his skill in manipulating people by his charms, physical and otherwise.

Although Reagan's stripped-down exposure began in the late 1930s, he continued to pose bare-chested and in shorts for fan magazine layouts well into the 1950s. Illustrating "stories" such as "Reagan's So Rugged" and "No Sad Songs for Ronnie," these spreads typically displayed photographs of him sweating while engaged in strenuous manual labor on his ranch. These beefcake poses, which placed a new emphasis on Reagan as a powerful man of action, were closer in spirit to Flynn's promotional campaign at Warner Brothers a decade earlier. Showing him at work rather than leisure, these photographs presented Reagan as a vigorous, energetic laborer caught in action. Captions for these stills used buzzwords such as "rough," "tough," and "ready." The posed photographs were calculated to present a naturally rugged outdoors man by shooting him mending fences, baling hay, watering animals, chopping wood, riding horses, or braving the elements. Other actors took on various fantasy personas to flex their muscles as sailors, fishermen, tennis bums, or gymnasts, often handling prop ropes, axes, and guns.

All of these photographs of Hollywood men in action were in the nineteenth-century tradition of Eadweard Muybridge (1830-1904), the father of the motion picture, who always posed men actively busy: carrying a boulder, sawing wood, jumping,

wrestling, or playing baseball. In contrast, Muybridge usually photographed his female subjects as passive or inactive. Work imagery of this type, of course, was far more prevalent in the U.S.S.R., especially in the socialist and trade union art of the nineteenth century. The dynamically muscular male bodies in these paintings display a primitive brute strength and are meant to symbolize the dignity and heroism of manual labor. It is ironic that the works of Soviet socialist realism bear such striking parallels to Hollywood image-making, of which Reagan was a part, in mid-twentieth-century America.

In the 1950s Reagan was competing with a whole new generation of Hollywood hunks such as Rock Hudson, Tony Curtis, George Nader, Jeff Chandler, Charleton Heston, Marlon Brando, Tab Hunter, and John Derek. By this time a new burgeoning physique culture had begun to emerge, and these heavy young dudes displayed a dedication to developing their bodies for their own sake: "Ars Gratia Artis." Reagan would have none of this, as he was still trying to emulate the more laid-back masculinity of John Wayne. Most of these actors faced another physique dilemma that Reagan did not have to worry about: to shave or not to shave their massive chests. In the past, the all-powerful censors of the Hayes Office had demanded smooth, hairless chests, as the unshaven chest was regarded as a source of moral corruption. With censorship restrictions beginning to loosen, this became a major problem for young male pin-ups and their studios. The airbrush continued to be used when the image-makers deemed it necessary, and the liberal application of oil to make muscular definition stand out became standard practice. As usual, the bronzed look could be supplied either by the hazy California sunshine or by Max Factor.

Reagan's personal role model was John Wayne, who had gone from football player to cowboy star; but he lacked Wayne's rugged macho quality. Other contemporaneous superstars proved to be more potent at the box office and edged Reagan out of the top echelon of stardom because of their unique celluloid personal chemistry: the daredevil dash of Errol Flynn, the toughness of Humphrey Bogart, the feistiness of James Cagney, the stalwart idealism of James Stewart, the laconic integrity of Gary Cooper, the debonair sophistication of Cary Grant, the 'savoir-faire' of Charles Boyer, the silky elegance of Tyrone Power, and the suave romanticism of Clark Gable. Each of these actors embodied on the screen some core set of American values and attitudes in a way that Reagan never quite approached. World War II interrupted Reagan's career for four years; when he returned to the screen in 1947, he faced stiff competition from scores of young actors such as Gregory Peck, Van Johnson, Peter Lawford, Robert Mitchum, Frank Sinatra, Tom Drake, Robert Walker, Gene Kelly, and Glenn Ford.

In the early 1950s, Reagan consciously modeled his look, clothes, and performances on those of his friend William Holden, even copying Holden's raised eyebrow cynical expression. Toward the end of the decade, as his features began to harden with middle age, Reagan was finally able to follow John Wayne and play crusty, tough western types. When eventually he played a role that was less than pretty and against the grain of all his previous parts in *The Killers*, it proved to be his final screen appearance and, incidentally, was the only film he made with Claude Akins, the younger Hollywood actor who most resembled him. However, playing a villain in this film had minimal effect on his nice-guy image.

Other contemporary actors made equally dramatic image switches which revitalized their movie careers. Dick Powell went from song-and-dance man to hard-boiled private eye, Robert Taylor from pretty-boy romantic leads to hard-bitten range rider, Richard Widmark from tough-guy villain to western and detective hero, Burt Lancaster from acrobatics to cerebral roles, and William Holden from breezy, young innocent to cynical man of the world. Instead of emulating any of these patterns, Reagan made the transition into television in the early 1950s, hosting three anthology series and acting in many dramatic shows.

During his first three years at Warner Brothers, Reagan had appeared in six films directed by Roy Enright, making more films with him than with any other director. Reagan also appeared in three films each with Lloyd Bacon and Lewis Foster, but none of these directors were of the first rank. In the remainder of his films, he never worked with the same director more than once or twice. Thus, he never had the opportunity to build a strong collaborative body of work with a master director in the tradition of great American filmmaking, such as John Wayne did with Howard Hawks and John Ford; James Stewart with Alfred Hitchcock and Frank Capra; Gary Cooper with Henry Hathaway and Sam Wood; James Cagney with Raoul Walsh; Errol Flynn with Michael Curtiz; Humphrey Bogart with John Huston; Spencer

Tracy with George Cukor and Stanley Kramer; Clark Gable with Victor Fleming and Clarence Brown; Henry Fonda with Fritz Lang and Ford; Tyrone Power with Henry King; and Cary Grant with Hawks, Hitchcock, and Cukor. Although most of Reagan's directors were not of world class reputation, he did manage to make a few films with such prestigious directors as Sam Wood, Michael Curtiz, Raoul Walsh, Don Siegel, Alan Dwan, and Edmund Goulding.

In terms of co-stars, Reagan appeared in seven films with Rosella Towne, six with Priscilla Lane, five each with Jane Wyman and Ann Sheridan, and four with Rhonda Fleming. The most frequent actors appearing in Reagan films were John Ridgely with 14 films, William Hopper with six, Wayne Morris with five, Alan Hale with five, and Dick Powell with four. In addition, several of his acting assignments found him in films with such Academy Award winners as Bette Davis, Olivia de Havilland, Ginger Rogers, Susan Hayward, Patricia Neal, Dorothy Malone, Humphrey Bogart, James Cagney, Broderick Crawford, Lee Marvin, Charles Coburn, and Van Heflin.

Ronald Reagan's first marriage (1940-1948) was to Jane Wyman, an Academy Award winner who was also under contract to Warner Brothers, for whom she made numerous films with actors who had appeared with Reagan. Wyman made a total of 76 films, 23 more than Reagan, and her successful TV series *Falcon Crest* kept her busy throughout the 1980s. Nancy Davis, his second wife, made most of her 11 films at Metro-Goldwyn-Mayer, and hence she and Reagan had fewer common co-stars. Only three actors and one actress appear in separate films with Reagan, Wyman, and Davis. Academy Award winner Charles Coburn appeared in *Kings Row* with Reagan, *Princess O'Rourke* with Wyman, and *The Doctor and the Girl* with Davis; Bruce Bennett, who had donned a loincloth to play Tarzan in the mid-1930s, was in *The Last Outpost* with Reagan, *Cheyenne* with Wyman, and *The Doctor and the Girl* with Davis; Warner Anderson was in

This Is the Army with Reagan, *The Blue Veil* with Wyman, and *The Doctor and the Girl* with Davis; Barbara Stanwyck was seen with Reagan in *Cattle Queen of Montana,* with Wyman in *Hollywood Canteen,* and with Davis in *East Side, West Side.*

Several of Reagan's Hollywood roles and associations presented intimations of his political future. In *This Is the Army,* the stage show his character had written was performed before the President of the United States in Washington. The film *Louisa,* which served as the pilot for the TV sitcom *December Bride,* was advertised with a print ad containing a picture of Reagan with the caption: "Dad lost his vice-presidency." In the *General Electric Theater* television drama "A Turkey for the President," co-starring Nancy Davis, he portrayed an American Indian poultry farmer whose son is chosen to send his pet bird to the White House for Thanksgiving. Ralph Bellamy, the actor who portrayed Franklin Delano Roosevelt in both stage and screen versions of *Sunrise at Campobello,* was in Reagan's film *Boy Meets Girl* and also in the television drama "Amos Burke: Who Killed Julie Greer?" on the *Dick Powell Show* with him. Reagan made two films, *Nine Lives Are Not Enough* and *Juke Girl,* with Faye Emerson, a fellow Warner Brothers contractee who later became the daughter-in-law of Roosevelt when she married his son Elliott. Reagan's anticommunist beliefs were rooted in Roosevelt's political philosophy. Shirley Temple, who co-starred with Reagan in *That Hagen Girl,* was appointed Ambassador to Ghana in 1974 by President Gerald Ford.

If actors John Wayne and William Holden were role models for Reagan's film career in the 1940s and 1950s, George Murphy was his exemplar for the transition from show business to politics. It is conceivable that without George Murphy, Ronald Reagan would never have become president, for it was the landslide election of Murphy to the United States Senate in 1964 that gave Reagan the credibility to run for governor of California in 1966. As the first Hollywood actor to break into the national political scene, Murphy paved the political road for Reagan. Nine years older than Reagan, Murphy had portrayed his father in *This Is the Army* and also had played Nancy Davis' husband in *Talk About a Stranger.*

Their lives have many parallels: ardent Democrats like their respective fathers, they switched to the Republican party where they sought and won high elected offices. In addition, they each served as president of the Screen Actors Guild, and both began film careers in the 1930s as light, two-dimensional actors, attempting tough-guy roles only after World War II. Further, they each became public relations spokesmen for corporations as a rehearsal for politics and also enjoyed the campaign advantage of revivals of their films on television. In addition, Murphy had a deep influence on Reagan's growing right-wing conservative viewpoint, thereby strengthening his sense of nationalism and patriotism. Reagan was an officer of the Screen Actors Guild from 1941-1960, including six terms as president from 1947-1952 and in 1959-1960. Murphy had been his immediate presidential predecessor from 1944-1946. Reagan was succeeded as president by Walter Pidgeon (1952-1957), who never sought higher office.

Among other Hollywood contemporaries who shared Reagan's conservative views were Walt Disney, Cecil B. DeMille, Sam Wood, Leo McCarey, Gary Cooper, Robert Taylor, Adolph Menjou, Barbara Stanwyck, Ginger Rogers, and Nancy Davis. Republican John Davis Lodge, who was a busy Hollywood actor in the 1930s, was elected governor of Connecticut in 1950 and subsequently served as ambassador to Spain under Eisenhower, to Argentina under Nixon, and to Switzerland under Reagan. Former screen actor of the 1950s and 1960s, John Gavin was appointed ambassador to

Mexico by Reagan early in his first administration. Another actor, Wendell Corey, who might be described as a second-string Reagan in the late 1940s and 1950s, was also an officer of the Screen Actors Guild, but he failed in his bid for nomination as Republican congressman, although he was later elected to the Santa Monica city council.

Throughout his two terms (1981-1989) as the 40th President of the United States, Ronald Reagan made constant references to his old celluloid Hollywood persona. With these frequent allusions to his past embodiments on film, Hollywood myth became Washington myth. He had already obtained considerable mileage out of "Where's the rest of me?," the line from *Kings Row* when he wakes up to discover that his legs had been needlessly amputated. This was used for the title of his (auto)biography, co-written in 1965 with Richard Hubler, to promote his campaign for the California governorship. While repeatedly using this quote throughout his presidential campaign and presidency, and even requesting that the film's theme music be played at his inauguration, his favorite movie line was "Win just one for the Gipper," that bit of half-time hokum from *Knute Rockne - All American* in which he portrayed George Gipp. One line that he delivered in *Storm Warning* has come back to haunt him: "If the people don't want federal government on their backs, the states are gonna hafta clean up their own mess."

These self-referential one-liners from his own films were augmented by lines from other old movies such as *Wing and a Prayer, State of the Union, The Bridges of Toko-Ri,* and *Shane,* as well as from more recent Hollywood efforts, particularly Clint Eastwood's *Dirty Harry* cycle and Sylvester Stallone's *Rocky* and *Rambo* films. His most strategic and effective film reference, however, was to George Lucas' 1977 *Star Wars,* whose science fiction fantasy weaponry helped Reagan to sell a large portion of the American public on the largest peacetime military build-up in the nation's history. "Star Wars" also has antecedents in one of his own early films, *Murder in the Air,* in which an "inertia projector" was invented to knock airplanes out of the sky by destroying their electrical systems. Reagan had discovered his identity in film with his first role, *Love Is on the Air,* fresh from radio station WHO in Des Moines, Iowa, portraying a radio announcer. Thus, at the very outset of his career, there was a blurring of distinction between art and life. As president, he approached issues in cinematic terms, used film analogies to make political points, and made no effort to distance himself from his celluloid self.

In 1954, the year in which he was to begin the most important and enduring association of his television career as jack-of-all-trades for General Electric, he made a transitional detour to Las Vegas, where he performed in a night club act at the Last Frontier Hotel. Reagan sang, danced, cracked jokes, performed slapstick routines and parodies of old film classics, and ended the act delivering a sentimental monologue on what it means to be an actor. The two-week engagement had been rehearsed at Ciro's night club in Hollywood and previewed at the Statler Hotel in downtown Los Angeles.

Under the tutelage of choreographer Pat Horn, he performed with Jay Moffett, Del Gleane, Benny Cruz, and Bob Garson. He shared the same bill with The Continentals, The Honey Brothers, The Blackburn Twins, The Adorabelles, and a chorus of semi-nude show girls. Although it turned out to be a one-time experience, he seriously considered bringing the act to the Waldorf-Astoria Hotel in New York. In the "Beer Garten" routine, he wore an apron advertising Pabst Blue Ribbon beer, donned a straw hat, sported a cane, and danced and sang, using a heavy, gutteral German accent. In another number with The Continentals, he did not sing but was the silent fifth member of a barbershop quartet and was shaved as he sat on a chair formed by the legs of two men in the group. They also performed an old-time baggy-pants vaudeville routine in which the five men raced around the stage hitting each other on the head with rolled-up newspapers.

At the beginning of the 1950s, Reagan made his first television appearance. While continuing to make feature films, he simultaneously appeared on television drama and variety programs, playing to a much wider audience than before. The major studios were then in the process of terminating the long-term contracts of most of their featured players. By the mid-1950s, with his films making poor showings at the box office, Reagan, too, had severed his contractual obligations with the film studios. In an era of diminishing feature film opportunities, Reagan was one of a handful of movie actors who obtained jobs hosting television dramatic "anthology" series. Those personalities who were deemed to have still potent box office appeal had their names included in the title of the series: Loretta Young, Robert Montgomery, Alfred Hitchcock, Jane Wyman, Barbara Stanwyck, June Allyson, and Douglas Fairbanks, Jr.

Although Reagan was not a part of this elite group, he successfully hosted three series and functioned in much the same way as other screen actors who doubled as hosts: Dick Powell (*Zane Grey Theater*), Merle Oberon (*Assignment Foreign Legion*), Joan Fontaine (*Family Classics*), Adolph Menjou (*Target*), Boris Karloff (*Thriller*), Burgess Meredith (*Big Story*), Maurice Evans (*Hall of Fame*), Dennis O'Keefe (*Suspicion*), Marvin Miller (*The Millionaire*), and John Conte (*Matinee Theater* and *TV Hour of Stars*). These actors, along with writer Rod Serling (*The Twilight Zone*), possessed the recognition factor that attracted viewers, but they were not in the superstar class in which naming the series for them was considered a commercial plus.

Robert Montgomery, the host, producer, and occasional star and director of *Robert Montgomery Presents*, which aired from 1950-1957, bears comparison to Reagan. Both were screen actors in the two decades before they entered television, and both served as presidents of the Screen Actors Guild, Montgomery's presidencies being 1935-1938 and 1946-1947. Robert Montgomery was an upper-bracket society type and was known for his sophisticated, white dinner jacket roles at Metro-Goldwyn-Mayer. He also directed five feature films between 1946 and 1960, becoming one of the first Hollywood actors to branch out in this way. In 1947 he headed the Hollywood Republican Committee to elect Thomas E. Dewey as president, and during the 1950s, he served President Dwight D. Eisenhower as "Special Consultant" on television and public communications. He was the first Hollywood actor to come this close to the Washington orbit of presidential power.

After first acting in several dramatic series, Reagan hosted his first TV program in 1953, *The Orchid Award,* which was also known as *The Orchid Room.* He hosted this ABC network program from Hollywood, alternating with Donald Woods from New York. The musical variety program of show business achievement had Reagan presenting the selected winners with an award — a real orchid. He would then interview the guest, and following a commercial break, the winners would perform their material. Award recipients included Rex Harrison, Lili Palmer, Eddie Fisher, Teresa Brewer, and Marguerite Piazza.

Reagan's most important and durable television work was as series host, occasional actor, and commercial spokesman for *General Electric Theater* from 1954-1962 on the CBS network. Functioning as roving goodwill ambassador for his sponsor, Reagan visited 135 General Electric plants across the country, addressing over a quarter of a million employees. These cheerleader speeches were protracted dress rehearsals for his entry into politics.

The dramatic anthology premiered in February of 1953, with no host for the first season. The program was broadcast on alternate weeks with *The Fred Waring Show* and began as a live drama; but eventually all of the episodes were filmed in advance, with Reagan as host and Ken Carpenter as announcer. The series was followed by a sequel, *General Electric True,* in the 1962-1963 seasons, with Jack Webb serving as host and narrator for stories that were based on actual incidents taken from the files of *True* magazine. One of the episodes Reagan hosted in 1961 was a pilot for the adventure series *Call to Danger,* which presented the exploits of a United States Treasury Department agent, portrayed by Lloyd Nolan. Reagan's final involvement in the series was that of producer of a two-part program that was broadcast in August of 1962. The drama entitled "My Dark Days" was based on the book *I Was a Spy* by Marion Miller; a southern California housewife played by Jeanne Crain joins the Communist party as an agent for the F.B.I. The first part, "Prelude," focused on Mrs. Miller's work in exposing the Communist party, while "Aftermath" presented her persecution and harassment by Communist sympathizers. As producer, Reagan was able to integrate his political ideology into his television work.

Reagan's last extended commercial television commitment was as host and actor for *Death Valley Days* in the 1965-1966 season. He participated in a total of 21 episodes, acting in eight of them and hosting 13. The series was sponsored by 20 Mule Team Borax (U.S. Borax & Chemical Corporation). *Death Valley Days* was the longest-running of all broadcast western dramas, beginning as a radio program from 1930-1945 on NBC Radio's Blue Network. It was then resurrected for television in 1952 with Stanley Andrews, "The Old Ranger," serving as host for 12 years prior to the Borax corporation's appointment of Reagan for seasons 13 and 14. Neil Reagan, an executive in the advertising firm of McCann-Erickson, which handled the program's production, was responsible for the company's hiring of his brother Ronald.

The series was an anthology of western stories depicting incidents in the lives of pioneers who lived, worked, and journeyed throughout the areas of Nevada and California in the latter half of the nineteenth century. The episodes focused on the struggle of their journeys and their problems in establishing a new homeland. It ran through an ad hoc syndicated network that carried it in exchange for advertising time. Reagan was succeeded as host by his good friend Robert Taylor (1966-1968), who was in turn succeeded by Dale Robertson (1968-1972). In the great Hollywood tradition of creative recycling or of warming over stale material, depending on your point of view, the episodes were subsequently syndicated with different hosts and series titles: Will Rogers, Jr. (*The Pioneers*), Ray Milland (*Trails West*), Rory Calhoun (*Western Star Theatre*), and John Payne (*The Call of the West*).

Reagan made his first professional appearance with his second wife, Nancy Davis (whom he married on March 4, 1952), on February 5, 1953 on NBC's *Ford Theater.* The drama was appropriately entitled "First Born" since Nancy had recently given birth, on October 22, 1952, to the first of their two children. Reagan and Davis subsequently appeared together on three *General Electric Theater* dramas: "Long Way 'Round" (1954), "A Turkey for the President" (1958), and "Money and the Minister" (1961), as well as in a *Zane Grey Theater* episode, "The Long Shadow," also in 1961. These five joint television appearances form a complement to their one film together, *Hellcats of the Navy* (1957).

Among his TV co-stars were three other actresses who also appeared with him in feature films: Angie Dickinson, Phyllis Thaxter, and Coleen Gray. In several of his roles, he was cast opposite such Academy Award-winning actresses as Geraldine Page, Anne Baxter, Ethel Barrymore, Kim Hunter, Cloris Leachman, and Teresa Wright. Additional TV co-stars included the following actresses: Jeanne Crain, Ann Blyth, Peggy Lee, Maureen O'Sullivan, Carolyn Jones, Agnes Moorehead, Carol Lynley, Carol Lawrence, Faye Wray, Eva Bartok, Nancy Guild, Paula Raymond, Kaye Thompson, and Barbara Billingsley. One of Reagan's most effective dramatic performances, "The Dark, Dark Hours," cast him opposite the gifted actor/rebel and cult hero James Dean (1931-1955), but he also appeared with such actors as Charles Bronson, Lee Marvin, David Janssen, Stephen Boyd, Gary Merrill, Francis X. Bushman, Kevin McCarthy, Charles Bickford, Brian Aherne, Raymond Massey, Francis L. Sullivan, Everett Sloane, Ward Bond, Sid Caesar, Scott Marlow, Dick Powell, Ralph Bellamy, Mickey Rooney, Lloyd Bridges, Jack Carson, Edgar Bergen, Dean Jones, and Nick Adams.

Although television is basically a producer's medium and film a director's medium, Reagan was directed on television by a number of quite competent directors who also worked in feature films. Most significantly, the actress/director/producer Ida Lupino directed him in three TV dramas. She had also come to television from motion pictures where she had starred in 59 films since 1933 and had directed seven films between 1949 and 1966. Other notable directors with whom he worked in television included Budd Boetticher, Ralph Nelson, Don Weis, James Neilsen, and Don Medford. In Reagan's television roles, more than in his films, he performed the adapted work of great writers such as Leo Tolstoy, Guy de Maupassant, Henrik Ibsen, Agatha Christie, Frank O'Connor, and Jessamyn West.

Under the equal-time rule for political candidates, TV reruns of *Death Valley Days* and *General Electric Theater* or any of Reagan's other TV and film appearances were barred from the air during the periods of his various candidacies.

Although Nancy Davis hit Hollywood 13 years after her future husband, she was groomed by Metro-Goldwyn-Mayer as a well-scrubbed, genteel-voiced, properly mannered, ingenue "lady" in the tradition of Ann Harding, Irene Dunne, Greer Garson, Teresa Wright, Dorothy McGuire, Jennifer Jones, and Deborah Kerr. The young Grace Kelly was simultaneously undergoing a similar, but higher-octane build-up on other Hollywood sound stages, and Marlon Brando and Marilyn Monroe were just beginning their screen careers. As a starlet and hopeful future MGM star, Davis possessed an aura of reserve, caution, sobriety, surface sophistication, slight haughtiness, and wistfulness. She as an unenthusiastic, somewhat bland young woman who could be easily shocked. Her heart-shaped face, with its sculpted chin, sharply featured nose, high forehead, and severe jaw, gave her an attractive yet somewhat antiseptic look. These were certainly not the qualities associated with the reigning queens of the lot — Lana Turner, Esther Williams, Judy Garland, Ava Gardner, and Elizabeth Taylor.

On the plus side, Nancy Davis had unusually large, wide-set, and expressive dark doe-eyes, which she instinctively knew how to use. Her eyes were her MGM trademark, conveying an expansive range of feeling — all positive traits such as sincerity, honesty, expectancy, hopefulness, empathy, and kindness. The widely spaced brown eyes seemed incapable of narrowing with malevolence or calculation. Many of the roles she was given

required her to be a wide-eyed, attentive listener as she gazed at her husband or fiance. Her eyes always registered a deep caring and indefatigable understanding of the other actors in the drama. In scene after scene, the cinematographer reduced her body to her face and then her face to her eyes in compelling close-ups. At the outset of her career at MGM, she was very self-conscious because she felt that her eyes were actually **too** large in proportion to her face. She soon learned that eyes could never be too large for the big screen, especially when they were so alive with pulchritude and intelligence.

Davis was coolly erotic, delicate, tasteful, modest, and dignified, possessing an elegant politesse. She had a freshly manicured prettiness, was serious, yet cheerful, and rarely displayed anger or extreme emotions. Apart from her marvelously dramatic eyes, she disciplined herself to project a severe economy of expression on the screen. She would never be accused of overacting. Davis was extremely well-groomed to the point of perfection, with every hair in place, makeup painstakingly applied, and her lustrous dark brown hair serving to soften her sharper facial planes.

The film footage of Davis in which she emoted under the guidance of George Cukor, the most important director with whom she worked, has never been seen by the public. Cukor directed her successful 1949 screen test for MGM in which she acted opposite new contractee Howard Keel. Keel went on to star in many successful films at MGM, including *Three Guys Named Mike* with Jane Wyman in 1951, and he succeeded Reagan, Walter Pidgeon, and Leon Ames as president of the Screen Actors Guild in 1958-1959. Davis' screen test was photographed by cinematographer George Folsey, and won her the standard seven-year contract with options. Arrangements for the test were facilitated through her connections with Loews' vice president Benjamin Thau and actors Spencer Tracy, Clark Gable, and Walter Huston. Davis had majored in drama at Smith College (class of 1943) and had appeared once on Broadway (*Lute Song*), in several road companies, and in one television drama prior to coming to Hollywood.

Davis was hard to pigeonhole, and the publicity department at MGM never really knew what to do with her. They could not seem to figure out how to mold her, or which image to go for. She certainly was not the overtly sexy, red-lipped, full-bosomed, glamorous seductress; besides, the studio already had Ava Gardner and Lana Turner, among others. Davis was not considered prime cheesecake material although, like her husband before her, she did pose for the obligatory bathing suit photographs. At the age of 27, she was considered too old to play the adolescent girl-next-door. These parts had formerly gone to June Allyson, Gloria De Haven, and Donna Reed, and were now being given to Davis' principal competition on the lot: Jane Powell, Debbie Reynolds, Janet Leigh, Leslie Caron, and Pier Angeli.

Studio powers tended to think of Davis in terms of Greer Garson and Deborah Kerr, patrician aristocratic types who also happened to be British. The problem with this image was that Davis was too American, so the studio compromised and cultivated for her an image of the very proper, homegrown, society lady from a good background on the right side of the tracks. She bore a physical resemblance to many dark-haired screen beauties, such as Kay Francis, Sylvia Sidney, Nancy Kelly, Ann Rutherford, Faye Wray, Luise Ranier, Rosalind Russell, Margaret Lockwood, Mary Astor, and Claudette Colbert. Had Davis continued her screen career beyond the nascent starlet phase, she might well be playing roles today that were once reserved for great character actresses such as Anne Revere, Estelle Winwood, Edna Mae Oliver, and Beulah Bondi.

Nancy Davis was the first professional actress to become First Lady of the United States. Like her husband, she tended to play American archetypes; her most frequent role was that of the self-possessed, average young wife or mother who was also often pregnant. Although her characters were perpetually in distress, she was a young woman in control of her feelings, a supportive there-when-you-need-her kind of gal. Her dark beauty helped to relieve the housewifely decorum and the dowdy frumpiness her roles customarily required. Playing women wearing aprons in pleasant domesticity, she could be counted on to lend a supportive shoulder when one was needed.

As with Reagan, her movie roles tended to echo her real life. Davis was the stepdaughter of Chicago neurosurgeon Loyal Davis, who had legally adopted her in 1935 when she was 14. Her brother Dr. Richard Davis is also a neurosurgeon in Philadelphia. In her first released film, *The Doctor and the Girl,* she played both the daughter and the sister of doctors (played by Charles Coburn and Glenn Ford, respectively). In her next release, actually the first film she made, *Shadow on the Wall,* Davis herself played a doctor, a psychiatrist working in the children's ward of a hospital. In *Donovan's Brain* she played the wife of a doctor who was acted by Lew Ayres. Davis had once been a volunteer nurse in a Chicago hospital and played one in *Hellcats of the Navy.*

She played the nice, young, middle-class wife in *The Next Voice You Hear* (her quintessential role) and in *Shadow in the Sky.* Her husband in both films was James Whitmore, who played an aircraft plant worker in the former and a garage owner in the latter. Davis also played a wife in *East Side, West Side;* she was the wife of California citrus grower George Murphy in *Talk About a Stranger,* and in *Crash Landing* she was Gary Merrill's Navy wife. She was engaged to John Hodiak in *Night Into Morning* and to Ronald Reagan in *Hellcats of the Navy.* Among the vocations she assumed were those of secretary (*East Side, West Side*), college professor (*Night Into Morning*), elementary teacher (*It's a Big Country*), and laboratory scientist (*Donovan's Brain*).

Davis worked with eleven separate directors in her eleven feature films in Hollywood. The most prestigious of these were William Wellman and Mervyn LeRoy. The latter allegedly arranged an introduction to her future husband. Wellman had previously directed Jane Wyman in *Magic Town,* and LeRoy had worked with her in three films: *Elmer the Great, The King and the Chorus Girl,* and *Fools for Scandal.*

The Doctor and the Girl was the film which had the most associations with Reagan and Wyman. Three of the actors, Charles Coburn, Bruce Bennett, and Warner Anderson, and the director, Curtis Bernhardt, had all made separate films with them at one time or another. Bernhardt had previously directed Reagan in *Million Dollar Baby* and *Juke Girl* and Wyman in *My Love Came Back,* and *The Blue Veil.*

Two Academy Award-winning best actors were cast opposite the young actress: Frederic March and Ray Milland. Milland had co-starred with Wyman in *The Lost Weekend* (his Oscar-winning role) and would re-team with her in *Let's Do It Again,* two years after completing the film with Davis. In addition, Davis' co-star Lew Ayres had acted opposite Wyman in her award-winning *Johnny Belinda.* Three actors in Davis' films had also appeared with Reagan: Van Heflin (*Santa Fe Trail*), George Murphy (*This Is the Army*), and Zachary Scott (*Stallion Road*). Rosemary De Camp appeared in one film with Davis and two with Reagan (*This Is the Army* and *Night unto Night*). De Camp was also the commercial spokeswoman for Reagan's *Death Valley Days.* Two actors, James Whitmore and Lewis Stone, starred in two films with Davis; although they were also both in *It's a Big Country,* they did not appear in the same episodes. Jean Hagen also made two films with Davis and became one of her closest friends on the Culver City lot.

Although Reagan had a 13-year head start over Davis in feature films, she made her television debut in 1949, a year before her future husband took that step. Subsequently, they jointly appeared in five television dramas, and Davis played in a total of 15 dramatic parts from 1949 through 1962. She was reunited with two of her film co-stars, Ray Milland and Gary Merrill (twice), and also appeared in television dramas with Academy Award-winners Charleton Heston and Lee Marvin, as well as other actors such as Dana Andrews, Ryan O'Neal, Steve Cochran, Richard Boone, John Ireland, Ward Bond, Willard Parker, Scott Marlow, Charles Aidman, and Art Linkletter. Although she was never known to date any of her film or television co-stars, she dated a number of actors before her marriage to Reagan, including Clark Gable, Robert Stack, Peter Lawford, and Robert Walker.

In 1952, the year Davis was released from her MGM contract, the studio went into a swift decline. In the same year she married Ronald Reagan, ten years her senior, and had her first child. From the day she married Reagan, she had but one obsession in life: her husband and his welfare. Her own political views were indistinguishable from his; she was in favor of military build-up, capital punishment, and nuclear power and was against the Equal Rights Amendment, abortion on demand, legalizing marijuana, and gun control. A woman of definite principles (the "Just say no" anti-drug program and the Foster Grandparent program) and strong, unshakable opinions, Davis was a vastly underrated actress.

The American public has been conditioned, over a period of 50 years, to look at visualizations of Ronald Reagan that are "picture perfect" — thousands of photographs, both still and moving as well as additional images on paper, tape, film, cassette, and disk. This endless stream of predictable media visuals is counter-balanced by a group of images that are handmade, contemplative, satiric, ironic, deliberative, analytical, multilayered, often disturbing and distorted, but above all, highly original. The images in the exhibition "Reagan: American Icon" cut through our previously conditioned perceptions and challenge us to see history in a far different way. No other person comes closer to representing the 1980s in this country or in the world than Ronald Reagan. The artists in the exhibition have discovered that, whatever their personal attitudes toward Reagan may be, his visual image is as potent as any other in this century.

Installation, Center Gallery, Bucknell University

Arneson, Robert
Ronny, 1986 (detail)
Glazed ceramic, wood, metal and various materials
47½ x 30½ x 26 ceramic head, 30 x 24 x 24 base
Frumkin/Adams Gallery

36

Arneson, Robert
26″ Model Ronny, 1986
Mixed media on paper, 68 x 46
Frumkin/Adams Gallery

Arneson, Robert
Ronny Portable, 1986
Bronze, 35½ x 21½ x 14
Struve Gallery, Chicago, Illinois

Brown, Roger
Presidential Portrait, 1985
Oil on canvas, 48 x 72 / outside 50 x 74
Phyllis Kind Gallery, Inc.

Brezinski, Edward
Nancy Reagan, 1984
Woodcut, 23 x 14¾ / outside 29 x 20
Private collection

Burson, Nancy
Warhead IV, 1985
Photo composite, 8⅛ x 6⅛ / outside 16 x 20
Holly Solomon Gallery

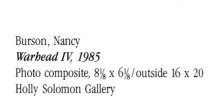

Castrucci, Andrew, in collaboration with Record
   Newspaper Art Department, New Jersey
I Love You Nancy Show, 1984
Acrylic, newspaper and spray paint on paper, 68 x 44
The artist

Castrucci, Andrew
I Love You Nancy Show, 1985
Oil on canvas, 30 x 70
The artist

40

Castrucci, Andrew
Ronnie The Wrestler, 1985
Oil on canvas, 80 x 66
The artist

Castrucci, Andrew
Cowboy, 1985
Oil on canvas, 78 x 64
The artist

Castrucci, Andrew
Portrait of Ronald Reagan, 1986
Oil on canvas, 14 x 11 / outside 20½ x 17½
The artist

41

Clarke, Richard
Ronald Reagan, 1986
Oil on panel, 43 x 60
The artist

Clarke, Richard
Fledgling Democracy, 1988
Oil on linen, 48 x 56
The artist

Cole, Peter
Postcard from Nicaragua, 1984
Mixed media on board, 14 x 47
The Gilbert and Lila Silverman Collection,
   Detroit, Michigan

Conal, Robbie
Ronald Reagan (Men with no lips)
Poster, based on painting
Paul Slansky

Conal, Robbie
Nancy Reagan (Women with teeth)
Poster, based on painting
Paul Slansky

Conal, Robbie
Contra Diction
Poster, based on painting
Paul Slansky

Dreiblatt, Jeffrey
Heaven Help Us, 1987
Prismacolor on paper, 23 x 28½ / outside 29 x 35
The artist

Ernst, Jimmy
Let Them Eat Jellybeans, 1981
Collage, 16 x 20 / outside 23 x 26
Dallas Ernst

Ernst, Jimmy
Let Them Eat Jellybeans, 1983
Collage, 10½ x 14½ / outside 14½ x 18½
Dallas Ernst

47

Glier, Mike
Give Blood, 1982
Oil on canvas, 93 x 120
The artist

48

Goodman, Sidney
A Day in the City, 1984-85
Oil on canvas, 67 x 83
Terry Dintenfass, Inc.

Goodman, Sidney
Three Men and a Pig, 1984-85
Charcoal, 37½ x 30½ / outside 44½ x 37½
Terry Dintenfass, Inc.

Grooms, Red
Nuclear Nuts, 1983
Painted enamel on wood, 22⅛ x 28⅜ x 10¾
The artist, courtesy of Marlborough Gallery

(detail)

Haacke, Hans
The Lord's Prayer (We Bring Good Things To Life), 1984
Color photograph, 29 x 41
John Weber Gallery

Haacke, Hans
We Bring Good Things To Life, 1983
Marbled wood pillar with fins, lettering, etched
  copper plate, gilt plaster bust, and circular
  fluorescent tube, overall height 110 x 35½; height
  of bust 27
John Weber Gallery

Haacke, Hans
Oelgemaelde, Hommage à Marcel Broodthaers, 1982
Installation; overall dimensions determined by
    exhibition space.
Oil painting in gold frame, picture lamp, brass
    plaque, brass stanchions with red velvet rope,
    red carpet, and photo mural. Painting, 35½ x 29
    including frame; carpet, 35 wide, length variable;
    brass plaque, 4½ x 12; photo mural, dimensions
    variable.
John Weber Gallery

52

Haacke, Hans
*The Safety Net (Proposal for Grand Central
    Station, New York), 1982*
Announcement for one-person exhibition, Bread
    and Roses Gallery, New York
John Weber Gallery

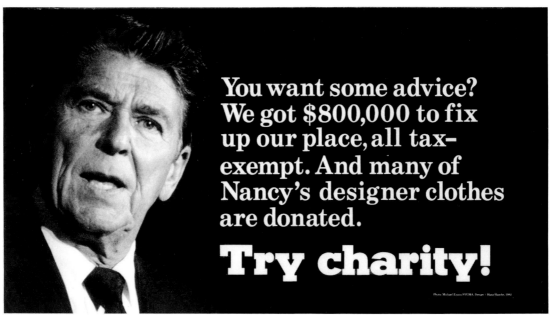

Haacke, Hans
*The Safety Net (Proposal for Grand Central
    Station, New York), 1982*
Light box and color transparency, 42 x 74 x 6½
John Weber Gallery

53

Haacke, Hans
Reaganomics, 1982
Color transparency in black wood frame; four
    fixtures with white fluorescent tubes, 72 x 49
John Weber Gallery

54

Haney, William L.
Wizard of Never, Never Land, 1985
Oil on canvas, 60½ x 60½
Capricorn Galleries, Bethesda, Maryland

Hofmekler, Ori
Charlie Chaplin
Tempera on board, 24 x 30
Jose Mussavi Gallery

Hofmekler, Ori
M.A.S.H.
Tempera on board, 19 x 20
Jose Mussavi Gallery

Hofmekler, Ori
Ronny II, 1984
Oil on board, 23 x 19 / outside 26 x 22
Jose Mussavi Gallery

Huffaker, Sandy
Bzzzt!, 1987
Oil on canvas, 10½ x 8½
Dr. and Mrs. Stanley B. Becker

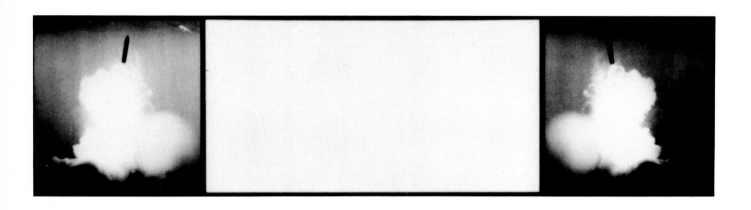

Jaar, Alfredo
Public Project, 1988
Durotran photographs in light boxes, 40 x 160 x 8
The artist

58

Komar & Melamid (Vitali Komar and Aleksandr
    Melamid)
Portrait of Ronald Reagan as a Centaur, 1981
Oil on canvas, 91 x 63
Michael H. Steinhardt

Kearns, Jerry
Repo Man, 1985
Acrylic on canvas, 84 x 94
Kent Fine Art

Kearns, Jerry
This Ain't No Disco, 1985
Acrylic on canvas, 84 x 94
Kent Fine Art

Kosalapov, Alexander
Hero, Leader, God, 1985
Oil on canvas, 42 x 70
The artist

Larson, Edward
Mad, 1985
Painted wood, 18¾ x 34½ x 4
Zolla/Lieberman Gallery, Chicago, Illinois

Leslie, Alfred
Ronald Reagan and Yuri Andropov, 1984
Oil on canvas, 60 x 54 / outside 63 x 59
The National Portrait Gallery, Smithsonian
Institution, Gift of Time, Inc.

64

McFadden, Leon
Ronald Reagan, 1982
Ink on museum board, 60 x 40
Alfred and Virginia Silbowitz

Marcus, Paul
Blowing It, 1986
Oil on wood, 24 x 18
P.P.O.W.

Marcus, Paul
The Foxhole, 1986
Watercolor on paper, 22 x 22¼ / outside 30½ x 28½
Private collection, P.P.O.W.

McKay, Wit
Bacon Reagan, 1983
Acrylic on canvas via computer jet plotter, 73 x 93
The artist

McKay, Wit
The State of the Union, 1982
Acrylic on canvas via computer jet plotter, 66 x 86
The artist

McKay, Wit
The Solution, 1983
Acrylic on canvas via computer jet plotter, 49 x 63,
   3 panels
The artist

Minter, Marilyn
Reagan Wallpaper, 1982
Silkscreen and enamel on board, 96 x 42, 3 panels
The artist

Prigov, Dimitri
Bestiale Series, 1-30, 1984 (detail)
Ink on paper
Elvehjem Museum of Art, University of Wisconsin-
    Madison, The Evjue Foundations Incorporated,
    Earl O. Vits Endowment, Bertha Ardt Plaenert
    Endowment, Frank J. Sensenbrenner Endowment
    and Art Collections Fund purchase

Rollins, Tim & K.O.S. (Kids of Survival)
From the Animal Farm (Ronald Reagan), 1984-87
Acrylic and wash on bookpages and linen, 26 x 20
Melvin D. Wolf

Sandlin, David
President Ronald Reagan as Charles III in
    Hunting Dress after Goya, 1985
Oil on masonite, 21 x 16½ / outside 31 x 27
Gracie Mansion Gallery

Sandlin, David
First Lady Nancy Reagan as the Marquesa
    De Pontejos after Goya, 1985
Oil on masonite, 21 x 16½ / outside 31 x 27
Gracie Mansion Gallery

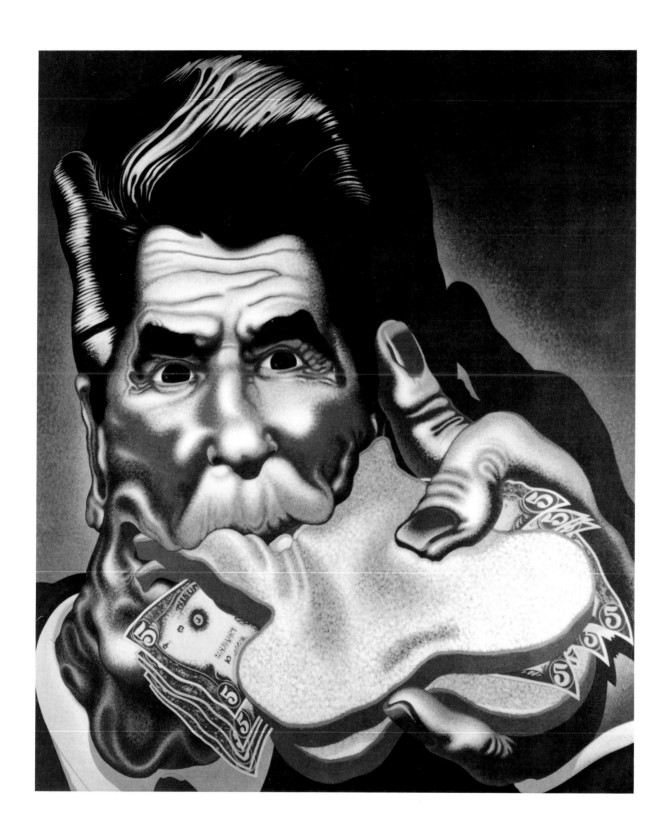

Saul, Peter
Ronald Reagan II, 1984
Oil, acrylic on canvas, 85 x 72½
Frumkin / Adams Gallery

Saul, Peter
Ronald Reagan #4 (Abortion), 1984
Alkyd on paper, 44¼ x 30 / outside 46 x 32
Frumkin / Adams Gallery

Saul, Peter
Ronald Reagan #5 (Tits), 1984
Alkyd on paper, 44¼ x 30 / outside 46 x 32
Frumkin / Adams Gallery

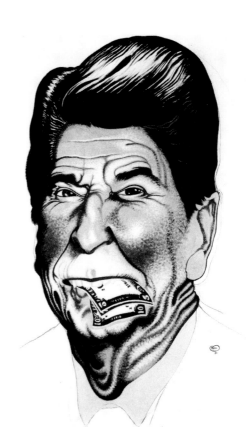

Saul, Peter
Ronald Reagan #3 (Lunch), 1984
Alkyd on paper, 44¼ x 30 / outside 46 x 32
Frumkin / Adams Gallery

Smith, Gregg
Reagan, 1985
Oil, acrylic on canvas, 42 x 40
The artist

74

Sivilli, Valerie A.
The Cancelling Out of Icons Reagan, 1987
Lithograph on paper, 29½ x 20½/outside 32¾ x 25
The artist

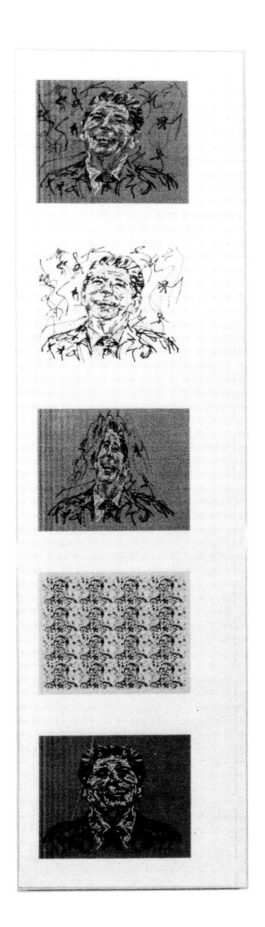

Smith, Gregg
Reagan, 1985
Computer drawing, 53 x 15
The artist

Van Dalen, Anton
Reagan Prison, 1982
Cutout with lit candle, 43 x 23 x 12½
Exit Art

Verona, Stephen
Ronald and Nancy Reagan, 1984
Acrylic on masonite, 72 x 42
The artist

77

Warhol, Andy
Van Heusen (Ronald Reagan), 1985
Screenprint, 38 x 38/outside 39½ x 39¼
Ronald Feldman Fine Art

Warhol, Andy
Van Heusen (Ronald Reagan), 1985
Acrylic on canvas, 22 x 22
Ronald Feldman Fine Art

Weegee (Arthur Felling)
For President Gov. Reagan, c. 1960
Photograph-silverprint, 8 x 10
Private collection

Wojarnowicz, David
Variation on Magritte's Bottle, 1984 (detail)
Mixed media, 8½ x 3¾
Robert and Mary Looker

Arneson, Robert
born 1930, Benicia, California; lives Benicia, California
Ronny, 1986 (detail)
Glazed ceramic, wood, metal and various materials
47½ x 30½ x 26 ceramic head, 30 x 24 x 24 base
Frumkin/Adams Gallery

Arneson, Robert
26" Model Ronny, 1986
Mixed media on paper, 68 x 46
Frumkin/Adams Gallery

Arneson, Robert
Ronny Portable, 1986
Bronze, 35½ x 21½ x 14
Struve Gallery, Chicago, Illinois

Brezinski, Edward
born 1954, Detroit, Michigan; lives New York City
Nancy Reagan, 1984
Woodcut, 23 x 14¾/outside 29 x 20
Private collection

Brown, Roger
born 1941, Hamilton, New York; lives Chicago, Illinois
Presidential Portrait, 1985
Oil on canvas, 48 x 72/outside 50 x 74
Phyllis Kind Gallery, Inc.

Burson, Nancy
born 1948, St. Louis, Missouri; lives New York City
Warhead IV, 1985
Photo composite, 8⅛ x 6⅛/outside 16 x 20
Holly Solomon Gallery

Castrucci, Andrew, in collaboration with Record
    Newspaper Art Department, New Jersey
born 1961, Englewood, New Jersey; lives New York City
I Love You Nancy Show, 1984
Acrylic, newspaper and spray paint on paper, 68 x 44
The artist

Castrucci, Andrew
Cowboy, 1985
Oil on canvas, 78 x 64
The artist

Castrucci, Andrew
Ronnie The Wrestler, 1985
Oil on canvas, 80 x 66
The artist

Castrucci, Andrew
I Love You Nancy Show, 1985
Oil on canvas, 30 x 70
The artist

Castrucci, Andrew
Portrait of Ronald Reagan, 1986
Oil on canvas, 14 x 11/outside 20½ x 17½
The artist

Clarke, Richard
born 1955, Newcastle, England; lives New York City
Ronald Reagan, 1986
Oil on panel, 43 x 60
The artist

Clarke, Richard
Fledgling Democracy, 1988
Oil on linen, 48 x 56
The artist

Cole, Peter
born 1946, Bairnsdale, Victoria, Australia; lives
    Innerlock, Australia
Postcard from Nicaragua, 1984
Mixed media on board, 14 x 47
The Gilbert and Lila Silverman Collection,
    Detroit, Michigan

Conal, Robbie
born 1944, New York City; lives Venice, California
Ronald Reagan (Men with no lips)
Poster, based on painting
Paul Slansky

Conal, Robbie
Nancy Reagan (Women with teeth)
Poster, based on painting
Paul Slansky

Conal, Robbie
Contra Diction
Poster, based on painting
Paul Slansky

Dreiblatt, Jeffrey
born 1961, Boulder, Colorado; lives Brooklyn, New York
Heaven Help Us, 1987
Prismacolor on paper, 23 x 28½/outside 29 x 35
The artist

Ernst, Jimmy
born 1920, Cologne, Germany; died 1984
Let Them Eat Jellybeans, 1981
Collage, 16 x 20/outside 23 x 26
Dallas Ernst

Ernst, Jimmy
Let Them Eat Jellybeans, 1983
Collage, 10½ x 14½/outside 14½ x 18½
Dallas Ernst

Glier, Mike
born 1953, Fort Thomas, Kentucky; lives Hoosick,
    New York
Give Blood, 1982
Oil on canvas, 93 x 120
The artist

Goodman, Sidney
born 1936, Philadelphia, Pennsylvania; lives
    New York City
A Day in the City, 1984-85
Oil on canvas, 67 x 83
Terry Dintenfass, Inc.

Goodman, Sidney
Three Men and a Pig, 1984-85
Charcoal, 37½ x 30½/outside 44½ x 37½
Terry Dintenfass, Inc.

Grooms, Red
born 1937, Nashville, Tennessee; lives New York City
Nuclear Nuts, 1983
Painted enamel on wood, 22⅛ x 28⅜ x 10¾
The artist, courtesy of Marlborough Gallery

Haacke, Hans
born 1936, Cologne, Germany; lives New York City
Oelgemaelde, Hommage à Marcel Broodthaers, 1982
Installation; overall dimensions determined by
    exhibition space.
Oil painting in gold frame, picture lamp, brass
    plaque, brass stanchions with red velvet rope,
    red carpet, and photo mural. Painting, 35½ x 29
    including frame; carpet, 35 wide, length variable;
    brass plaque, 4½ x 12; photo mural, dimensions
    variable.
John Weber Gallery

Haacke, Hans
*The Safety Net (Proposal for Grand Central
    Station, New York), 1982*
Light box and color transparency, 42 x 74 x 6½
John Weber Gallery

Haacke, Hans
*The Safety Net (Proposal for Grand Central
    Station, New York), 1982*
Announcement for one-person exhibition, Bread
    and Roses Gallery, New York
John Weber Gallery

Haacke, Hans
Reaganomics, 1982
Color transparency in black wood frame; four
    fixtures with white fluorescent tubes, 72 x 49
John Weber Gallery

Haacke, Hans
We Bring Good Things To Life, 1983
Marbled wood pillar with fins, lettering, etched
    copper plate, gilt plaster bust, and circular
    fluorescent tube, overall height 110 x 35½; height
    of bust 27
John Weber Gallery

Haacke, Hans
*The Lord's Prayer (We Bring Good Things To
    Life), 1984*
Color photograph, 29 x 41
John Weber Gallery

Haney, William L.
born 1939, Strong City, Kansas; lives Louisville,
    Kentucky
Wizard of Never, Never Land, 1985
Oil on canvas, 60½ x 60½
Capricorn Galleries, Bethesda, Maryland

Hofmekler, Ori
born 1952, Israel; lives New York City
Ronny II, 1984
Oil on board, 23 x 19/outside 26 x 22
Jose Mussavi Gallery

Hofmekler, Ori
M.A.S.H.
Tempera on board, 19 x 20
Jose Mussavi Gallery

Hofmekler, Ori
Charlie Chaplin
Tempera on board, 24 x 30
Jose Mussavi Gallery

Huffaker, Sandy
born 1943, Chattanooga, Tennessee; lives Princeton,
    New Jersey
Bzzzt!, 1987
Oil on canvas, 10½ x 8½
Dr. and Mrs. Stanley B. Becker

Jaar, Alfredo
born 1956, Santiago, Chile; lives New York City
Public Project, 1988
Durotran photographs in light boxes, 40 x 160 x 8
The artist

Kearns, Jerry
born 1943, Petersburg, Virginia; lives New York City
Repo Man, 1985
Acrylic on canvas, 84 x 94
Kent Fine Art

Kearns, Jerry
This Ain't No Disco, 1985
Acrylic on canvas, 84 x 94
Kent Fine Art

Komar & Melamid (Vitali Komar and Aleksandr
    Melamid)
born 1943 and 1945, Moscow, U.S.S.R.; live New
    York City
Portrait of Ronald Reagan as a Centaur, 1981
Oil on canvas, 91 x 63
Michael H. Steinhardt

Kosalapov, Alexander
born 1943, Moscow, U.S.S.R.; lives New York City
Hero, Leader, God, 1985
Oil on canvas, 42 x 70
The artist

Larson, Edward
born 1931, Chaplin, Missouri; lives Chicago, Illinois
Mad, 1985
Painted wood, 18¾ x 34½ x 4
Zolla/Lieberman Gallery, Chicago, Illinois

Leslie, Alfred
born 1927, New York City; lives Amherst,
    Massachusetts
Ronald Reagan and Yuri Andropov, 1984
Oil on canvas, 60 x 54/outside 63 x 59
The National Portrait Gallery, Smithsonian
    Institution, Gift of Time, Inc.

Marcus, Paul
born 1953, Bronx, New York; lives New York City
The Foxhole, 1986
Watercolor on paper, 22 x 22¼/outside 30½ x 28½
Private collection, P.P.O.W.

Marcus, Paul
Blowing It, 1986
Oil on wood, 24 x 18
P.P.O.W.

McFadden, Leon
born 1920, St. Paul, Minnesota; lives Yreka,
    California
Ronald Reagan, 1982
Ink on museum board, 60 x 40
Alfred and Virginia Silbowitz

McKay, Wit
born 1956, Ann Arbor, Michigan; lives New York City
The State of the Union, 1982
Acrylic on canvas via computer jet plotter, 66 x 86
The artist

McKay, Wit
The Solution, 1983
Acrylic on canvas via computer jet plotter, 49 x 63,
    3 panels
The artist

McKay, Wit
Bacon Reagan, 1983
Acrylic on canvas via computer jet plotter, 73 x 93
The artist

Minter, Marilyn
born 1949, Shreveport, Louisiana; lives New York City
Reagan Wallpaper, 1982
Silkscreen and enamel on board, 96 x 42, 3 panels
The artist

Prigov, Dimitri
born 1940, Moscow, U.S.S.R; lives Moscow,
    U.S.S.R.
Bestiale Series, 1-30 (Detail), 1984
Ink on paper
Elvehjem Museum of Art, University of Wisconsin-
    Madison, The Evjue Foundations Incorporated,
    Earl O. Vits Endowment, Bertha Ardt Plaenert
    Endowment, Frank J. Sensenbrenner Endowment
    and Art Collections Fund purchase

Rollins, Tim & K.O.S. (Kids of Survival)
born 1955, St. Paul, Minnesota; lives New York City
From the Animal Farm (Ronald Reagan), 1984-87
Acrylic and wash on bookpages and linen, 26 x 20
Melvin D. Wolf

Sandlin, David
born 1956, Belfast, Northern Ireland; lives New
    York City
*President Ronald Reagan as Charles III in
    Hunting Dress after Goya, 1985*
Oil on masonite, 21 x 16½/outside 31 x 27
Gracie Mansion Gallery

Sandlin, David
*First Lady Nancy Reagan as the Marquesa
    De Pontejos after Goya, 1985*
Oil on masonite, 21 x 16½/outside 31 x 27
Gracie Mansion Gallery

Saul, Peter
born 1934, San Francisco, California; lives Austin, Texas
Ronald Reagan II, 1984
Oil, acrylic on canvas, 85 x 72½
Frumkin/Adams Gallery

Saul, Peter
Ronald Reagan #3 (Lunch), 1984
Alkyd on paper, 44¼ x 30/outside 46 x 32
Frumkin/Adams Gallery

Saul, Peter
Ronald Reagan #5 (Tits), 1984
Alkyd on paper, 44¼ x 30/outside 46 x 32
Frumkin/Adams Gallery

Saul, Peter
Ronald Reagan #4 (Abortion), 1984
Alkyd on paper, 44¼ x 30/outside 46 x 32
Frumkin/Adams Gallery

Sivilli, Valerie A.
born 1959, Brooklyn, New York; lives Brooklyn,
   New York
The Cancelling Out of Icons, 1987
Lithograph on paper, 29½ x 20½/outside 32¾ x 25
The artist

Sivilli, Valerie A.
The Cancelling Out of Icons II, 1987
Lithograph on paper, 29½ x 20½/outside 32¾ x 25
The artist

Sivilli, Valerie A.
The Cancelling Out of Icons Reagan, 1987
Lithograph on paper, 29½ x 20½/outside 32¾ x 25
The artist

Smith, Gregg
born 1951, Easton, Pennsylvania; lives New
   York City
Reagan, 1985
Computer drawing, 53 x 15
The artist

Smith, Gregg
Reagan, 1985
Oil, acrylic on canvas, 42 x 40
The artist

Van Dalen, Anton
born 1938, Amstelveen, Holland; lives New York City
Reagan Prison, 1982
Cutout with lit candle, 43 x 23 x 12½
Exit Art

Verona, Stephen
born 1940, Springfield, Illinois; lives Bel Air,
   California
Ronald and Nancy Reagan, 1984
Acrylic on masonite, 72 x 42
The artist

Warhol, Andy
born 1931, Pittsburgh, Pennsylvania; died 1987
Van Heusen (Ronald Reagan), 1985
Acrylic on canvas, 22 x 22
Ronald Feldman Fine Art

Warhol, Andy
Van Heusen (Ronald Reagan), 1985
Screenprint, 38 x 38/outside 39½ x 39¼
Ronald Feldman Fine Art

Weegee (Arthur Felling)
born 1899, Zolczew, Poland; died 1968
For President Gov. Reagan, c. 1960
Photograph-silverprint, 8 x 10
Private collection

Wojarnowicz, David
born 1954, Red Bank, New Jersey; lives New York City
Variation on Magritte's Bottle, 1984
Mixed media, 8½ x 3¾
Robert and Mary Looker

(All dimensions are indicated in inches.)

	☆ *Parallel Film Developments*	
	Ronald Reagan	*Nancy Davis*
1932		
1933		
1934		
1935		
1936		
1937	Love Is on the Air	
	Hollywood Hotel	
1938	Swing Your Lady	
	Sergeant Murphy	
	Accidents Will Happen	
	Cowboy from Brooklyn	
	Boy Meets Girl	
	Girls on Probation	
	Brother Rat	
1939	Going Places	
	Secret Service of the Air	
	Dark Victory	
	Code of the Secret Service	
	Naughty but Nice	
	Hell's Kitchen	
	Angels Wash Their Faces	
	Smashing the Money Ring	

Jane Wyman	Best Picture
The Kid from Spain	Grand Hotel
Elmer the Great	Cavalcade
College Rhythm	It Happened One Night
Rumba All the King's Horses Stolen Harmony King of Burlesque	Mutiny on the Bounty
My Man Godfrey Stage Struck Cain and Mabel Polo Joe Smart Blonde Gold Diggers of 1937	The Great Ziegfeld
The King and the Chorus Girl Ready, Willing and Able Slim The Singing Marine Mr. Dodd Takes the Air Public Wedding	The Life of Emile Zola
The Spy Ring Fools for Scandal He Couldn't Say No Wide Open Faces The Crowd Roars Brother Rat	You Can't Take It with You
Tailspin The Kid from Kokomo Torchy Plays with Dynamite Private Detective Kid Nightingale	Gone with the Wind

☆ Parallel Film Developments

	Ronald Reagan	Nancy Davis
1940	Brother Rat and a Baby An Angel from Texas Murder in the Air Knute Rockne - All American Santa Fe Trail Tugboat Annie Sails Again	
1941	The Bad Man Million Dollar Baby Nine Lives Are Not Enough International Squadron	
1942	Kings Row Juke Girl Desperate Journey	
1943	This is the Army	
1944		
1945		
1946		
1947	Stallion Road That Hagen Girl The Voice of the Turtle	
1948		
1949	John Loves Mary Night unto Night The Girl from Jones Beach It's a Great Feeling	The Doctor and the Girl East Side, West Side

Jane Wyman	Best Picture
Brother Rat and a Baby An Angel from Texas Flight Angels My Love Came Back Gambling on the High Seas Tugboat Annie Sails Again	Rebecca
Bad Men of Missouri Honeymoon for Three The Body Disappears You're in the Army Now	How Green Was My Valley
Larceny, Inc. My Favorite Spy Footlight Serenade	Mrs. Miniver
Princess O'Rourke	Casablanca
Make Your Own Bed Crime by Night The Doughgirls Hollywood Canteen	Going My Way
The Lost Weekend	The Lost Weekend
One More Tomorrow Night and Day The Yearling	The Best Years of Our Lives
Cheyenne	Gentlemen's Agreement
Johnny Belinda	Hamlet
A Kiss in the Dark The Lady Takes a Sailor It's a Great Feeling	All the King's Men

☆ *Parallel Film Developments*

	Ronald Reagan	*Nancy Davis*
1950	The Hasty Heart Louisa	Shadow on the Wall The Next Voice You Hear...
1951	Storm Warning Bedtime for Bonzo The Last Outpost	Night Into Morning
1952	Hong Kong She's Working Her Way Through College The Winning Team	It's a Big Country Shadow in the Sky Talk About a Stranger
1953	Tropic Zone Law and Order	Donovan's Brain
1954	Prisoner of War Cattle Queen of Montana	
1955	Tennessee's Partner	
1956		
1957	Hellcats of the Navy	Hellcats of the Navy
1958		Crash Landing
1959		

Jane Wyman	*Best Picture*
Stage Fright The Glass Menagerie	All About Eve
Three Guys Named Mike Here Comes the Groom The Blue Veil Starlift	An American in Paris
The Will Rogers Story Just for You	The Greatest Show on Earth
Let's Do It Again So Big	From Here to Eternity
Magnificent Obsession	On the Waterfront
Lucy Gallant All That Heaven Allows	Marty
Miracle in the Rain	Around the World in 80 Days
	The Bridge on the River Kwai
	Gigi
Holiday for Lovers	Ben-Hur

☆ *Parallel Film Developments*

	Ronald Reagan	*Nancy Davis*
1960		
1961		
1962		
1963		
1964	The Killers	
1965		
1966		
1967		
1968		
1969		

Jane Wyman	Best Picture*
Pollyanna	The Apartment
	West Side Story
Bon Voyage	Lawrence of Arabia
	Tom Jones
	My Fair Lady
	The Sound of Music
	A Man for All Seasons
	In the Heat of the Night
	Oliver!
How to Commit Marriage	Midnight Cowboy

*A complete list of the Academy Award best pictures is contained in the following "Oscar Story":

It happened one night in the heat of the night that Rocky, an American in Paris, and the French connection, Gigi, went to the Grand Hotel in Casablanca while on a trip around the world in 80 days and were shown how green was my valley by my fair lady who was going my way and while it was all quiet on the western front the platoon led by Patton crossed the bridge on the River Kwai where they heard the sound of music, a Broadway melody from the greatest show on earth by Amadeus; all this occurred while they were spending the lost weekend listening to Kramer vs. Kramer with three other couples: Marty and Annie Hall, Rebecca and the godfather Ben-Hur, Mrs. Miniver and the godfather II Lawrence of Arabia, along with his sons Oliver and Tom Jones; then they all made a gentlemen's agreement not to reveal the west side story which Gandhi, a man for all seasons, had told the great Ziegfeld about the life of Emile Zola and all about Eve-with-wings; the one flew over the cuckoo's nest on chariots of fire flying out of Africa from here to eternity after being convinced by Hamlet and all the king's men that you can't take it with you because it's gone with the wind; at sunrise, awakened by the sting, this cavalcade arrived with terms of endearment at the apartment on the waterfront where they had spent the best years of their lives with the last emperor, rain man, and ordinary people observing the mutiny on the bounty, led by the deer hunter, a midnight cowboy from Cimarron.

🖺 *Parallel Television Developments*

	Ronald Reagan	Nancy Davis
1949		The Philco Television Playhouse
1950	Burns and Allen Amm-I-Dent Show The Nash Airflyte Theater	
1951		
1952	Hollywood Opening Night	
1953	Ford Theater Schlitz Playhouse of the Stars The Orchid Award Chrysler Medallion Theater B.F. Goodrich Lux Video Theater Revlon Mirror Theater	Ford Theater Schlitz Playhouse of the Stars
1954	Schlitz Playhouse of the Stars General Electric Theater Ford Theater Lux Video Theater Operation Entertainment	Schlitz Playhouse of the Stars General Electric Theater
1955	General Electric Theater	Climax!
1956	General Electric Theater The Judy Garland Show	General Electric Theater
1957	General Electric Theater	
1958	General Electric Theater	General Electric Theater
1959	General Electric Theater	

Jane Wyman	Highest Rating
	Texaco Star Theater
	Arthur Godfrey's Talent Scouts
	I Love Lucy
	I Love Lucy
	I Love Lucy
General Electric Theater Fireside Theater	The $64,000 Question
Jane Wyman Theater	I Love Lucy
Jane Wyman Theater	Gunsmoke
	Gunsmoke
Lux Playhouse	Gunsmoke

Parallel Television Developments

	Ronald Reagan	Nancy Davis
1960	General Electric Theater The June Allyson Show The Swingin' Years	General Electric Theater
1961	General Electric Theater Dick Powell's Zane Grey Theater The Bob Hope Show The Dick Powell Show	General Electric Theater Dick Powell's Zane Grey Theater Tall Man
1962	General Electric Theater	Wagon Train The Dick Powell Theater 87th Precinct
1963	Wagon Train	
1964	Kraft Suspense Theater News Special Death Valley Days	
1965	Death Valley Days	
1966	Death Valley Days	
1967	The Joey Bishop Show	
1968	CBS Reports	

Jane Wyman	Highest Rating*
Checkmate	Gunsmoke
General Electric Theater Investigators Rawhide The Bob Hope Show	Wagon Train
Wagon Train	The Beverly Hillbillies
Naked City	The Beverly Hillbillies
	Bonanza
	Bonanza
	Bonanza
	The Andy Griffith Show
	Rowan & Martin's Laugh-In

*A complete list of the highest rated television shows is contained in the following ''A.C. Nielson Story'':

A bonanza of happy days awaited the Beverly Hillbillies dynasty: Andy Griffith, Bill Cosby, and Arthur Godfrey when they saw gunsmoke and, keeping it all in the family, boarded the wagon train for Dallas with Rowan & Martin and Laverne & Shirley to attend the Texaco Star Theater for 60 minutes where Marcus Welby, M.D. answered the $64,000 question: I Love Lucy.

Ronald Reagan

Feature Films

1937

Love Is on the Air (a.k.a. **The Radio Murder Mystery; Inside Story**). Warner Bros./First National.
Director: Nick Grinde. Writers: Morton Grant, George Bricker. Producer: Bryan Foy.
Cast: Eddie Acuff, Robert Barrat, June Travis, Willard Parker, William Hopper.

Hollywood Hotel. Warner Bros./First National.
Director: Busby Berkeley. Writers: Jerry Wald, Leo and Richard Macauley. Producer: Hal B. Wallis.
Cast: Dick Powell, Rosemary Lane, Lola Lane, Louella Parsons, Frances Langford, Glenda Farrell, Susan Hayward, Carole Landis, Benny Goodman, Raymond Paige, Allyn Joslyn, Hugh Herbert, Ted Healy, Grant Mitchell, Eddie Acuff, Perc Westmore, Alan Mowbray, Edgar Kennedy, John Ridgely.

1938

Swing Your Lady. Warner Bros.
Director: Ray Enright. Writers: Joseph Schrank, Maurice Leo. Producers: Samuel Bischoff, Hal B. Wallis.
Cast: Humphrey Bogart, Frank McHugh, Louise Fazenda, Penny Singleton, Nat Pendleton, the Weaver Brothers, Allen Jenkins, Irving Bacon.

Sergeant Murphy. Warner Bros.
Director: B. Reeves Eason. Writer: William Jacobs. Producer: Bryan Foy.
Cast: Mary Maguire, Donald Crisp, Rosella Towne.

Accidents Will Happen. Warner Bros.
Director: William Clemens. Writers: George Bricker, Anthony Coldeway. Producer: Bryan Foy.
Cast: Gloria Blondell, Dick Purcell, Willard Parker, Sheila Bromley.

Cowboy from Brooklyn (a.k.a. **Romance and Rhythm**). Warner Bros.
Director: Lloyd Bacon. Writer: Earl Baldwin. Producers: Lou Edelman, Hal B. Wallis.
Cast: Dick Powell, Pat O'Brien, Priscilla Lane, Ann Sheridan, Rosella Towne, Jeffrey Lynn, Dick Foran, James Stephenson, John Ridgely, Hobart Cavanaugh.

Boy Meets Girl. Warner Bros.
Director: Lloyd Bacon. Writers: Sam and Bella Spewack. Producers: George Abbott, Hal B. Wallis, Sam Bischoff.
Cast: James Cagney, Pat O'Brien, Marie Wilson, Ralph Bellamy, Penny Singleton, Carole Landis, Rosella Towne, Dick Foran, Frank McHugh, James Stephenson, John Ridgely.

Girls on Probation. Warner Bros./First National.
Director: William McGann. Writer: Crane Wilbur. Producer: Bryan Foy.
Cast: Jane Bryan, Anthony Averill, Sheila Bromley, Susan Hayward, Henry O'Neill, Sig Rumann.

Brother Rat. Warner Bros./First National.
Director: William Keighley. Writers: Richard Macaulay, Jerry Wald. Producers: Robert Lord, Hal B. Wallis. Cinematography: Ernest Haller.
Cast: Wayne Morris, Priscilla Lane, Eddie Albert, Jane Wyman, Jane Bryan, Louise Beavers, Don DeFore, Henry O'Neill.

1939

Going Places. Warner Bros./Cosmopolitan.
Director: Ray Enright. Writers: Jerry Wald, Sig Herzig, Maurice Leo. Producer: Hal B. Wallis.
Cast: Dick Powell, Anita Louise, Allen Jenkins, Thurston Hall, Eddie Anderson, Rosella Towne, Ward Bond, Louis Armstrong, Maxine Sullivan, John Ridgely.

Secret Service of the Air. Warner Bros.
Director: Noel Smith. Writer: Raymond Schrock. Producer: Bryan Foy.
Cast: John Litel, James Stephenson, Eddie Foy Jr., Rosella Towne, John Ridgely, Anthony Averill.

Dark Victory. Warner Bros./First National.
Director: Edmund Goulding. Writer: Casey Robinson. Producer: Hal B. Wallis. Music: Max Steiner. Cinematography: Ernest Haller.
Cast: Bette Davis, George Brent, Humphrey Bogart, Geraldine Fitzgerald, Henry Travers, Cora Witherspoon, Rosella Towne, John Ridgely.

Code of the Secret Service. Warner Bros.
Director: Noel Smith. Writers: Lee Katz, Dean Franklin. Producer: Bryan Foy.
Cast: Rosella Towne, Eddie Foy Jr.

Naughty but Nice. Warner Bros.
Director: Ray Enright. Writers: Jerry Wald, Richard Macaulay. Producer: Sam Bischoff.
Cast: Dick Powell, Gale Page, Ann Sheridan, ZaSu Pitts, Jerry Colonna, Helen Broderick, Allen Jenkins, Maxie Rosenbloom, Peter Lind Hayes, Grady Sutton, Hobart Cavanaugh, Halliwell Hobbes, John Ridgely, Vera Lewis.

Hell's Kitchen. Warner Bros.
Directors: Lewis Seiler, E.A. Dupont. Writers: Crane Wilbur, Fred Niblo Jr. Producers: Mark Hellinger, Bryan Foy.
Cast: Grant Mitchell, Stanley Fields, Margaret Lindsay, the Dead End Kids, Charles Foy.

Angels Wash Their Faces. Warner Bros. Sequel to Angels with Dirty Faces (1938).
Director: Ray Enright. Writers: Michael Fessier, Niven Busch, Robert Buckner. Producer: Robert Fellows.
Cast: Ann Sheridan, the Dead End Kids, Bonita Granville, Margaret Hamilton, Marjorie Main, Grady Sutton, Henry O'Neill, John Ridgely.

Smashing the Money Ring (a.k.a. Queer Money). Warner Bros.
Director: Terry Morse. Writers: Anthony Coldeway, Raymond Schrock. Producer: Bryan Foy.
Cast: Margot Stevenson, Eddie Foy Jr., John Ridgely.

1940

Brother Rat and a Baby (a.k.a. Baby Be Good). Warner Bros. Sequel to Brother Rat (1938).
Director: Ray Enright. Writers: John Monks Jr., Fred F. Finklehoffe. Producers: Robert Lord, Hal B. Wallis.
Cast: Wayne Morris, Priscilla Lane, Eddie Albert, Jane Wyman, Jane Bryan, Arthur Treacher, Mayo Methot, Alan Ladd, Paul Harvey, Irving Bacon.

An Angel from Texas. Warner Bros.
Director: Ray Enright. Writers: Fred Niblo Jr., Bertram Millhauser. Producer: Robert Fellows.
Cast: Eddie Albert, Wayne Morris, Jane Wyman, Rosemary Lane, Eddie Acuff, John Litel, Hobart Cavanaugh.

Murder in the Air. Warner Bros.
Director: Lewis Seiler. Writer: Raymond Schrock. Producer: Bryan Foy.
Cast: John Litel, James Stephenson, Eddie Foy Jr., Lya Lys.

Knute Rockne — All American. Warner Bros.
Director: Lloyd Bacon. Writer: Robert Buckner. Producer: Hal B. Wallis.
Cast: Pat O'Brien, Gale Page, Donald Crisp, John Litel, John Qualen, John Sheffield, George Reeves, Henry O'Neill, John Ridgely, Albert Basserman, Dorothy Tree, Tex Swan, William Hopper.

Tugboat Annie Sails Again. Warner Bros. Sequel to Tugboat Annie (1933).
Director: Lewis Seiler. Writer: Walter De Leon. Producer: Bryan Foy.
Cast: Marjorie Rambeau, Alan Hale, Jane Wyman, Chill Wills, Neil Reagan.

Santa Fe Trail. Warner Bros./First National.
Director: Michael Curtiz. Writer: Robert Buckner. Producers: Hal B. Wallis, Robert Fellows. Music: Max Steiner.
Cast: Errol Flynn, Olivia de Havilland, Raymond Massey, Alan Hale, William Lundigan, Van Heflin, John Litel, Ward Bond, Susan Peters (Carnahan), Henry O'Neill, Hobart Cavanaugh, Guinn Williams, William Hopper, Nestor Paiva.

1941

The Bad Man (a.k.a. Two-Gun Cupid). Metro-Goldwyn-Mayer.
Director: Richard Thorpe. Writer: Wells Root. Producer: J. Walter Ruben.
Cast: Wallace Beery, Lionel Barrymore, Laraine Day, Henry Travers, Chill Wills, Tom Conway.

Million Dollar Baby (a.k.a. Miss Wheelright Discovers America). Warner Bros.
Director: Curtis Bernhardt. Writers: Casey Robinson, Richard Macaulay, Jerry Wald. Producers: Hal B. Wallis, David Lewis.
Cast: Priscilla Lane, Jeffrey Lynn, May Robson, Lee Patrick, John Qualen, Johnny Sheffield, Charles Drake, John Ridgely, Irving Bacon.

Nine Lives Are Not Enough. Warner Bros.
Director: A. Edward Sutherland. Writer: Fred Niblo Jr. Producer: William Jacobs.
Cast: Joan Perry, James Gleason, Faye Emerson, Howard da Silva, Charles Drake, Thurston Hall, John Ridgely.

International Squadron. Warner Bros.
Director: Lothar Mendes. Writers: Barry Trivers, Kenneth Gamet. Producer: Edmund Grainger.
Cast: James Stephenson, Olympe Bradna, William Lundigan, Joan Perry, Helmut Dantine, Julie Bishop, John Ridgely, Reginald Denny, William Hopper.

1942

Kings Row. Warner Bros.
Director: Sam Wood. Writer: Casey Robinson. Producer: Hal B. Wallis. Music: Erich Wolfgang Korngold. Cinematography: James Wong Howe.
Cast: Ann Sheridan, Robert Cummings, Charles Coburn, Betty Field, Claude Rains, Judith Anderson, Nancy Coleman, Maria Ouspenskaya, Harry Davenport, Scotty Beckett.

Juke Girl. Warner Bros.
Director: Curtis Bernhardt. Writers: A.I. Bezzerides, Kenneth Gamet. Producers: Hal B. Wallis, Jerry Wald, Jack Saper.
Cast: Ann Sheridan, Richard Whorf, George Tobias, Gene Lockhart, Alan Hale, Howard da Silva, Faye Emerson, Dewey Robinson, Fuzzy Knight, William Hopper, Ray Teal.

Desperate Journey (a.k.a. **Forced Landing**). Warner Bros./First National.
Director: Raoul Walsh. Writer: Arthur T. Horman. Producers: Hal B. Wallis, Jack Saper. Music: Max Steiner.
Cast: Errol Flynn, Raymond Massey, Nancy Coleman, Alan Hale, Arthur Kennedy, Helmut Dantine, Ferdinand Schumann-Heink, Albert Basserman, Sig Rumann, William Hopper.

1943

This Is the Army. Warner Bros.
Director: Michael Curtiz. Writers: Casey Robinson, Claude Binyon, Irving Berlin. Producers: Jack L. Warner, Hal B. Wallis.
Cast: George Murphy, Joan Leslie, George Tobias, Alan Hale, Charles Butterworth, Rosemary De Camp, Dolores Costello, Una Merkel, Kate Smith, Joe Louis, Frances Langford, Gertrude Niesen, Ezra Stone, Victor Moore, Ruth Donnelly, Irving Bacon, Warner Anderson.

1947

Stallion Road. Warner Bros.
Director: James V. Kern. Writer: Stephen Longstreet. Producer: Alex Gottlieb.
Cast: Alexis Smith, Zachary Scott, Harry Davenport, Peggy Knudsen, Dewey Robinson, Monte Blue.

That Hagen Girl. Warner Bros.
Director: Peter Godfrey. Writer: Charles Hoffman. Producer: Alex Gottleib. Music: Franz Waxman. Cinematography: Karl Freund.
Cast: Shirley Temple, Rory Calhoun, Lois Maxwell, Conrad Janis, Penny Edwards, Jean Porter, Harry Davenport.

The Voice of the Turtle (a.k.a. **One for the Books**). Warner Bros.
Director: Irving Rapper. Writer: John Van Druten. Producer: Charles Hoffman. Music: Max Steiner.
Cast: Eleanor Parker, Eve Arden, Wayne Morris, Kent Smith, Philip Morris, Nino Pepitone.

1949

John Loves Mary. Warner Bros.
Director: David Butler. Writers: Phoebe and Henry Ephron. Producer: Jerry Wald.
Cast: Patricia Neal, Jack Carson, Wayne Morris, Edward Arnold, Virginia Field, Paul Harvey, Irving Bacon, Nino Pepitone.

Night unto Night. Warner Bros.
Director: Don Siegel. Writer: Kathryn Scola. Producer: Owen Crump. Music: Franz Waxman.
Cast: Viveca Lindfors, Broderick Crawford, Rosemary De Camp, Osa Massen, Craig Stevens, Irving Bacon.

The Girl from Jones Beach. Warner Bros.
Director: Peter Godfrey. Writer: I.A.L. Diamond. Producer: Alex Gottlieb.
Cast: Virginia Mayo, Eddie Bracken, Dona Drake, Henry Travers, Lois Wilson, Florence Bates, Jerome Cowan, Helen Westcott, Paul Harvey, Dale Robertson, Jeff Richards, Lola Albright, Joi Lansing, Joan Vohs, Myrna Dell, Betty Underwood.

It's a Great Feeling. Warner Bros.
Director: David Butler. Writers: Jack Rose, Melville Shavelson. Producer: Alex Gottlieb.
Cast: Jackson Carson, Dennis Morgan, Doris Day, Errol Flynn, Gary Cooper, Joan Crawford, Sydney Greenstreet, Danny Kaye, Patricia Neal, Eleanor Parker, Edward G. Robinson, Jane Wyman, David Butler, Michael Curtiz, King Vidor, Raoul Walsh, Bill Goodwin, Nina Talbot, Joan Vohs, Maureen Reagan, Claire Carleton, Jacqueline De Witt, Irving Bacon.

1950

The Hasty Heart. Warner Bros.
Director: Vincent Sherman. Writer: Ranald Mac Dougall. Producers: Howard Lindsay, Russell Crouse.
Cast: Richard Todd, Patricia Neal, Anthony Nicholis, Howard Crawford, Alfred Bass.

Louisa. Universal.
Director: Alexander Hall. Writer: Stanley Roberts. Producer: Robert Arthur.
Cast: Charles Coburn, Ruth Hussey, Edmund Gwenn, Spring Byington, Piper Laurie, Scotty Beckett, Martin Milner, Connie Gilchrist.

1951

Storm Warning. Warner Bros.
Director: Stuart Heisler. Writers: Daniel Fuchs, Richard Brooks. Producer: Jerry Wald.
Cast: Ginger Rogers, Doris Day, Steve Cochran, Ned Glass, King Donovan, Dewey Robinson, Gene Evans.

Bedtime for Bonzo. Universal.
Director: Frederick de Cordova. Writers: Val Burton, Lou Breslow. Producer: Michel Kraike.
Cast: Dianna Lynn, Walter Slezak, Jesse White.

The Last Outpost. Paramount.
Director: Lewis R. Foster. Writers: Geoffrey Homes, George Worthing Yates, Winston Miller. Producers: William H. Pine, William C. Thomas.
Cast: Rhonda Fleming, Bruce Bennett, Bill Williams, Noah Beery Jr., Peter Hanson, John Ridgely.

1952

Hong Kong. Paramount.
Director: Lewis R. Foster. Writer: Winston Miller. Producers: William H. Pine, William C. Thomas.
Cast: Rhonda Fleming, Nigel Bruce, Danny Chang, Marvin Miller, Lady May Lawford.

She's Working Her Way Through College. Warner Bros.
Director: H. Bruce Humberstone. Writer: Peter Milne. Producer: William Jacobs.
Cast: Virginia Mayo, Gene Nelson, Don DeFore, Phyllis Thaxter, Patrice Wymore, Eve Miller, The Blackburn Twins.

The Winning Team. Warner Bros.
Director: Lewis Seiler. Writers: Ted Sherdeman, Seeleg Lester, Mervin Gerard. Producer: Bryan Foy.
Cast: Doris Day, Frank Lovejoy, Russ Tamblyn, Eve Miller.

1953

Tropic Zone. Paramount.
Director/Writer: Lewis R. Foster. Producers: William H. Pine, William C. Thomas.
Cast: Rhonda Fleming, Estelita, Noah Beery Jr., Grant Withers.

Law and Order. Universal.
Director: Nathan Juran. Writers: John and Owen Bagni, D.D. Beauchamp. Producer: John W. Rogers.
Cast: Dorothy Malone, Alex Nicol, Preston Foster, Dennis Weaver, Jack Kelly.

1954

Prisoner of War. Metro-Goldwyn-Mayer.
Director: Andrew Marton. Writer: Allen Rivkin. Producer: Henry Berman.
Cast: Steve Forrest, Dewey Martin, Oscar Homolka, Robert Horton, Harry Morgan, Darryl Hickman, Paul Stewart, Jerry Paris, John Lupton, Stuart Whitman.

Cattle Queen of Montana. RKO/Filmcrest.
Director: Allan Dwan. Writers: Robert Blees, Howard Estabrook. Producer: Benedict Borgeaus.
Cast: Barbara Stanwyck, Gene Evans, Lance Fuller, Anthony Caruso, Jack Elam, Yvette Dugay.

1955

Tennessee's Partner. RKO/Filmcrest.
Director: Allan Dwan. Writers: D.D. Beauchamp, Graham Baker, Milton Krims, Teddi Sherman. Producer: Benedict Borgeaus.
Cast: John Payne, Rhonda Fleming, Coleen Gray, Angie Dickinson, Anthony Caruso, Leo Gordon.

1957

Hellcats of the Navy. Columbia.
Director: Nathan Juran. Writers: David Lang, Raymond Marcus. Producer: Charles H. Schneer.
Cast: Nancy Davis, Arthur Franz, Robert Arthur, William Leslie.

1964

The Killers. NBC-TV
Director/Producer: Don Siegel. Writer: Gene L. Coon. Music: John Williams.
Cast: Lee Marvin, John Cassavetes, Angie Dickinson, Clu Gulager, Claude Akins, Norman Fell, Seymour Cassel.

Documentaries (and Short Subjects)

1941

How to Improve Your Golf
Cast: Jane Wyman.

1942

Mr. Gardenia Jones (U.S. Army)

1943

Rear Gunner (U.S. Army/WB)
Writer: Edwin Gilbert.
Cast: Burgess Meredith.

Hollywood in Uniform (Columbia)
Cast: Clark Gable, Tyrone Power, James Stewart, Alan Ladd, John Payne.

1944

For God and Country (U.S. Army)

1948

OK for Pictures (Warner Bros.)

So You Want To Be in Pictures (Joe MacDoakes)

Studio Tour (Warner Bros.)

1966

Mr. Kennedy, Mr. Reagan, and the Big Beautiful Beleaguered American Dream (Canadian Broadcasting Corporation)
Narrator: Philip Deane.

1976

It's Showtime (a.k.a. The Wonderful World of Those Cuckoo Crazy Animals), (United Artists)
Producers: Fred Weintraub, Paul Heller.
Cast: Charlie Chaplin, John Wayne, Bing Crosby, Humphrey Bogart, Cary Grant, Elizabeth Taylor, Mae West, Errol Flynn, Betty Grable, James Cagney, Gregory Peck, Myrna Loy, Ray Milland, Irene Dunne, William Powell, Mickey Rooney, Gene Autry, Joan Blondell, Van Johnson, Dick Powell, Buster Crabbe, Roddy McDowall, Penny Singleton, Arthur Lake, Walter Slezak.

Narration

1938

The Amazing Dr. Clitterhouse (Warner Bros.)
Director: Anatole Litvak. Writers: John Huston, John Wexley. Producer: Robert Lord.
Cast: Edward G. Robinson, Clair Trevor, Humphrey Bogart, Gale Page, Donald Crisp, Allen Jenkins, Thurston Hall, John Litel, Vladimir Sokoloff, Henry O'Neill, Maxie Rosenbloom, Ward Bond.

1942

Behind the Line of Duty (U.S. Army)

1944

Target Tokyo (U.S. Army)

1961

The Young Doctors (United Artists — Drexel/Miller-Turman)
Director: Phil Karlson. Writer: Joseph Hayes. Producers: Lawrence Turman, Stuart Miller.
Cast: Frederic March, Ben Gazzara, Dick Clark, Ina Ballin, Eddie Albert, Edward Andrews, Aline MacMahon, Arthur Hill, Rosemary Murphy, Barnard Hughes, James Broderick, Gloria Vanderbilt, George Segal, Matt Crowley, Dick Button, Phyllis Love, Joseph Bova.

1963

The Truth About Communism

1965

Let the World Go Forth
Co-narrator: Robert Taylor.

Unrealized Film Projects
(Indicating actor who played the role)

1941

They Died with Their Boots On (Warner Bros.) With Errol Flynn.
Director: Raoul Walsh.

1943

Casablanca (Warner Bros.) With Humphrey Bogart.
Director: Michael Curtiz.

1948
The Treasure of Sierra Madre (Warner Bros.) With Tim Holt.
Director: John Huston.

1949
The Stratton Story (Metro-Goldwyn-Mayer) With James Stewart.
Director: Sam Wood.

1950
Rocky Mountain (a.k.a. Ghost Mountain) (Warner Bros.) With Errol Flynn.
Director: William Keighley.

Woman in Hiding (Universal-International) With Howard Duff.
Director: Michael Gordon.

1952
Bonzo Goes to College (Universal-International) With Charles Drake.
Director: Frederick de Cordova. Sequel to "Bedtime for Bonzo."

1953
She's Back on Broadway (Warner Bros.) With Steve Cochran.
Director: Gordon Douglas. Sequel to "She's Working Her Way Through College."

Appearance Removed from Final Print

1937
Submarine D-1 (Warner Bros./First National)
Director: Lloyd Bacon. Writers: Frank Wead, Warren Duff, Lawrence Kimble. Producer: Lou Edelman.
Cast: Pat O'Brien, George Brent, Wayne Morris, Broderick Crawford, Doris Weston, Frank McHugh, Henry O'Neill, Veda Ann Borg, Dennis Moore.

Film Song Titles

1937
Hollywood Hotel
Hooray for Hollywood; Can't Teach My Heart New Tricks; I'm Like a Fish Out of Water; I've Hitched My Wagon to a Star; Let That Be a Lesson to You; Silhouetted in the Moonlight; Sing, You Son of a Gun.

1938
Swing Your Lady
Mountain Swingaroo; Hillbilly from Tenth Avenue; The Old Apple Tree; Swing Your Lady; Dig Me a Grave in Missouri.

Cowboy from Brooklyn
I've Got a Heartful of Music; I'll Dream Tonight; Ride, Tenderfoot, Ride; Cowboy from Brooklyn.

Boy Meets Girl
With a Pain in My Heart.

1939
Going Places
Jeepers Creepers; Say It with a Kiss; Oh, What a Horse was Charley.

Naughty but Nice
Hooray for Spinach; Corn Pickin'; I'm Happy About the Whole Thing; In a Moment of Weakness; I Don't Believe in Signs.

1943
This is the Army
God Bless America; Oh, How I Hate To Get Up in the Morning; This is the Army, Mr. Jones; The Army's Made a Man Out of Me; I'm Getting Tired So I Can Sleep; What the Well Dressed Man in Harlem Will Wear; I Left My Heart at the Stage-Door Canteen; Give a Cheer for the Navy; American Eagles; Poor Little Me I'm on K.P.

1952
She's Working Her Way Through College
I'll Be Loving You; The Stuff That Dreams Are Made Of; Give 'Em What They Want; Am I in Love?; Love Is Still for Free; She's Working Her Way Through College; With Plenty of Money and You.

The Winning Team
Take Me Out to the Ball Game; I'll String Along with You; Lucky Day; Ain't We Got Fun.

1955
Tennessee's Partner
Heart of Gold.

Remake Sources and Successors

1937

Love Is on the Air was a remake of the following:

Hi Nellie! (1934) Warner Bros.

Director: Mervyn LeRoy. Writers: Abem Finkel, Sidney Sutherland. Based on a story by Roy Chanslor. Producer: Robert Presnell.

Cast: Paul Muni, Glenda Farrell, Ned Sparks, Hobart Cavanaugh, Douglass Dumbrille, Robert Barrat.

Love Is on the Air was remade as the following:

You Can't Escape Forever (1942) Warner Bros.

Director: Jo Graham. Writers: Fred Niblo Jr., Hector Chevigny. Producer: Mark Hellinger.

Cast: George Brent, Brenda Marshall, Gene Lockhart, Paul Harvey, Roscoe Karns, Erville Alderson, Edward Cianelli.

The House Across the Street (1949) Warner Bros.

Director: Richard Bare. Writer: Russell Hughes. Producer: Saul Elkins.

Cast: Wayne Morris, Janis Page, Alan Hale, James Mitchell, Barbara Bates, Bruce Bennett, James Holden, Ray Montgomery.

1938

Brother Rat was remade as the following:

About Face (1952) Warner Bros.

Director: Roy Del Ruth. Writer: Peter Milne. Based on the play by John Monks Jr. and Fred F. Finklehoffe. Producer: William Jacobs.

Cast: Gordon MacRae, Eddie Bracken, Dick Wessen, Phyllis Kirk, Virginia Gibson, Joel Grey, Aileen Stanley Jr., Larry Keating.

1939

Going Places was a remake of the following:

The Hottentot (1923) First National.

Based on the play by Victor Mapes and Willie Collier.

The Hottentot (1929) Warner Bros.

Director: Roy Del Ruth. Writer: Harvey Threw.

Cast: Edward Everett Horton, Patsy Ruth Miller, Douglas Gerrard.

Dark Victory was remade as the following:

Stolen Hours (1963) United Artists / Mirisch-Barbican

Director: Daniel Petrie. Writer: Jessamyn West. Based on the play by George Emerson Brewer Jr. and Bertran Bloch. Producer: Dennis Holt.

Cast: Susan Hayward, Michael Craig, Edward Judd, Diane Baker, Paul Rogers.

Hell's Kitchen was a remake of the following:

The Mayor of Hell (1933) Warner Bros.

Director: Archie Mayo. Writer: Edward Chodorov. Based on the story by Islin Auster. Producer: Lucian Hubbard.

Cast: James Cagney, Frankie Darro, Madge Evans, Dudley Digges, Allen Jenkins, Hobart Cavanaugh.

Crime School (1938) Warner Bros. / First National.

Director: Lewis Seiler. Writers: Crane Wilbur, Vincent Sherman. Producer: Bryan Foy.

Cast: Humphrey Bogart, the Dead End Kids, Gale Page.

Smashing the Money Ring was a remake of the following:

Jailbreak (1930) Warner Bros. / First National.

Director: Mervyn LeRoy. Writers: Al Cohn, Henry McCarthy. Based on the play "Jailbreak" by Dwight Taylor.

Cast: Conrad Nagel, Raymond Hackett, Ralph Ince, Bernice Claire, Tully Marshall, William Holden, Fred Howard.

Jailbreak (a.k.a. **Murder in the Big House**) (1936) Warner Bros.

Director: Nick Grinde. Writers: Robert D. Andrews, Joseph Hoffman. Producer: Bryan Foy.

Cast: Dick Purcell, Craig Reynolds, June Travis, Barton MacLane, Eddie Acuff, Joseph King, Addison Richards.

Smashing the Money Ring was remade as the following:

Murder in the Big House (a.k.a. **Born for Trouble**) (1942) Warner Bros.

Director: B. Reeves Eason. Writer: Raymond Schrock. Producer: William Jacobs.

Cast: Van Johnson, Faye Emerson, Ruth Ford, George Meeker, Frank Wilcox, Michael Ames.

1940

An Angel from Texas was a remake of the following:

The Butter and Egg Man (1928) Warner Bros. / First National.

Director: Richard Wallace. Based on the play by George S. Kaufman.

Cast: Jack Mulhall.

The Tenderfoot (1932) Warner Bros.

Director: Ray Enright. Writers: Earl Baldwin, Monty Banks, Arthur Caesar.

Cast: Joe E. Brown, Ginger Rogers, Lew Cody, Vivienne Oakland, Robert Greig.

Hello Sweetheart (1935) Warner Bros. / Teddington.

Director: Monty Banks.

Cast: Claude Hulbert, Gregory Ratoff, Jane Carr.

Dance, Charlie, Dance (1937) Warner Bros. / First National.

Director: Frank McDonald. Writers: Crane Wilbur, William Jacobs. Producer: Bryan Foy.

Cast: Stuart Irwin, Jean Muir, Glenda Farrell, Allen Jenkins, Addison Richards, Charles Foy.

An Angel from Texas was remade as the following:
Three Sailors and a Girl (1953) Warner Bros.
Director: Roy Del Ruth. Writers: Roland Kibbee, Devery Freeman. Producer: Sammy Kahn.
Cast: Jane Powell, Gordon MacRae, Gene Nelson, Jack E. Leonard, Sam Levine, Veda Ann Borg.

1941

The Bad Man was a remake of the following:
The Bad Man (1923) First National.
Director: Edwin Carewe. Based on the play by Holbrook Blinn and a story by Porter Emerson Brown and C.H. Towne.
Cast: Enid Bennett, Holbrook Blinn.
The Bad Man (1930) Warner Bros./First National.
Director: Clarence Badger. Writer: Howard Egtabrook.
Cast: Walter Huston, Sidney Blackmer, Dorothy Revier, James Rennie, O.P. Heggie.
West of Shanghai (1937) Warner Bros./First National.
Director: John Farrow. Writer: Crane Wilbur. Producer: Bryan Foy.
Cast: Boris Karloff, Ricardo Cortez, Sheila Bromley, Vladimir Sokoloff, Beverly Roberts, Gordon Oliver, Richard Loo, Luke Chan.

International Squadron was a remake of the following:
Ceiling Zero (1936) Warner Bros.
Director: Howard Hawks. Writer: Frank Wead. Based on the play by Frank Wead. Producer: Harry Joe Brown.
Cast: James Cagney, Pat O'Brien, June Travis, Stuart Erwin, Isabel Jewell, Barton MacLane, Craig Reynolds, Henry Wadsworth, Martha Tibbetts, Maryon Curtiz.

1952

She's Working Her Way Through College was a remake of the following:
The Male Animal (1942) Warner Bros.
Director: Elliott Nugent. Writers: Julius J. and Philip G. Epstein, Stephen Morehouse Avery. Based on the play by James Thurber and Elliott Nugent. Producers: Hal B. Wallis, Wolfgang Reinhardt.
Cast: Henry Fonda, Olivia de Havilland, Jack Carson, Joan Leslie, Eugene Pallette, Don De Fore, Herbert Anderson.

1953

Law and Order was a remake of the following:
Law and Order (1932) Universal.
Director: Edward Cahn. Writers: John Huston, Tom Reed. Based on the novel "Saint Johnson" by William R. Burnett.
Cast: Walter Huston, Harry Carey, Ralph Ince, Andy Devine, Dewey Robinson, Walter Brennan.
Law and Order (1940) Universal.
Director: Ray Taylor. Writer: Sherman Lowe.
Cast: Johnny Mack Brown, Fuzzy Knight, Nell O'Day, James Craig, Bob Baker.

1955

Tennessee's Partner was a remake of the following:
Tennessee's Partner (1916) Lasky/Paramount.
Based on the short story by Bret Harte. Producer: Jesse L. Lasky.
Cast: Fannie Ward.
The Flaming Forties (1924) Producers Distributing Corporation.
Director: Tom Forman. Producer: Hunt Stromberg.
Cast: Harry Carey.

1964

The Killers was a remake of the following:
The Killers (1946) Universal.
Director: Robert Siodmak. Writer: Anthony Veiller. Based on the short story by Ernest Hemingway. Producer: Mark Hellinger.
Cast: Burt Lancaster, Ava Gardner, Edmond O'Brien, Albert Dekker, Sam Levene, Charles McGraw, William Conrad, Jeff Corey, Virginia Christine.

Literary Sources

Plays

Cowboy from Brooklyn — ''Howdy, Stranger'' by Robert Sloane, Louis Pelletier Jr.

Boy Meets Girl by Bella and Sam Spewack.

Brother Rat by John Monks Jr., Fred F. Finklehoffe.

Going Places — ''The Hottentot'' by Victor Mapes, William Collier Sr.

Dark Victory by George Emerson Brewer Jr., Bertram Black.

An Angel from Texas — ''The Butter and Egg Man'' by George S. Kaufman.

International Squadron — ''Ceiling Zero'' by Frank Wead.

The Bad Man by Holbrook Blinn.

This Is the Army — ''Yip, Yip, Yaphank'' by Irving Berlin.

The Voice of the Turtle by John Van Druten.

John Loves Mary by Norman Krasna.

The Hasty Heart by John Patrick.

She's Working Her Way Through College — ''The Male Animal'' by James Thurber, Elliot Nugent.

Novels

Nine Lives Are Not Enough by Jerome Odlum.

Kings Row by Henry Bellamann.

Stallion Road by Stephen Longstreet.

That Hagen Girl by Edith Roberts.

Night Unto Night by Philip Wylie.

Biographies

Knute Rockne, All American — George Gipp, Notre Dame University football team.

The Winning Team — Grover Cleveland Alexander, St. Louis Cardinals baseball team.

Short Stories

Tennessee's Partner by Bret Harte.

The Killers by Ernest Hemingway.

[The remainder of his films.]

Film Genres

Action/Adventure

Secret Service of the Air, Code of the Secret Service, Smashing the Money Ring, Murder in the Air, Angels Wash Their Faces, Hong Kong, Tropic Zone, The Killers.

Western

The Bad Man, Santa Fe Trail, The Last Outpost, Law and Order, Cattle Queen of Montana, Tennessee's Partner.

Military

Sergeant Murphy, International Squadron, Desperate Journey, The Hasty Heart, Prisoner of War, Hellcats of the Navy.

Comedy

Boy Meets Girl, Brother Rat, Brother Rat and a Baby, An Angel from Texas, Tugboat Annie Sails Again, Million Dollar Baby, The Voice of the Turtle, John Loves Mary, The Girl from Jones Beach, It's a Great Feeling, Louisa, Bedtime for Bonzo.

Musical

Hollywood Hotel, Swing Your Lady, The Cowboy from Brooklyn, Going Places, Naughty but Nice, This Is the Army, She's Working Her Way Through College.

Melodrama

Accidents Will Happen, Love Is on the Air, Girls on Probation, Hell's Kitchen, Dark Victory, Knute Rockne—All American, Nine Lives Are Not Enough, Kings Row, Juke Girl, Stallion Road, That Hagen Girl, Night Unto Night, Storm Warning, The Winning Team.

Roles Played: Vocations

Entertainment/Art/Media

Radio announcer — Love Is on the Air, Hollywood Hotel, Swing Your Lady, Boy Meets Girl.

Newspaper reporter — Nine Lives Are Not Enough.

Broadway producer — An Angel from Texas.

Press agent — Cowboy from Brooklyn.

Music publisher — Naughty but Nice.

Concert pianist — Million Dollar Baby.

Magazine illustrator — The Girl from Jones Beach.

Architect — Louisa.

Actor (himself) — It's a Great Feeling.

Military

Army — Sergeant Murphy, Santa Fe Trail, Desperate Journey, This Is the Army, The Voice of the Turtle, John Loves Mary, The Hasty Heart, The Last Outpost, Cattle Queen of Montana.
Navy — Hellcats of the Navy.
Air Force — International Squadron.
Cadet — Brother Rat, Brother Rat and a Baby.
Government volunteer — Prisoner of War.
Ex-GI soldier of fortune — Hong Kong.

Law Enforcement

F.B.I. Secret Service agent — Secret Service of the Air, Code of the Secret Service, Smashing the Money Ring, Murder in the Air.
District attorney — Girls on Probation, Storm Warning.
Son of district attorney — Angels Wash Their Faces.
Lawyer — That Hagen Girl.
Marshall — Law and Order.

Outdoor Labor

Itinerant fruit picker — Juke Girl.
Banana plantation foreman — Tropic Zone.
Railroad worker — Kings Row.
Sailor — Tugboat Annie Sails Again.
Cowboy — The Bad Man, Tennessee's Partner.

Indoor Work

Insurance adjuster — Accidents Will Happen.
Social worker — Hell's Kitchen.
College professor — She's Working Her Way Through College.

Athletics

Football player — Knute Rockne—All American.
Baseball player — The Winning Team.

Science

Veterinary surgeon — Stallion Road.
Biochemist — Night Unto Night.
Psychology professor — Bedtime for Bonzo.

Unemployed

Playboy — Dark Victory, Going Places.
Crook — The Killers.

Co-workers (and number of films together)

Directors

Lloyd Bacon (3), Busby Berkeley (1), Curtis Bernhardt (2), David Butler (2), William Clemens (1), Michael Curtiz (2), Frederick de Cordova (1), Allan Dwan (2), E.A. Dupont (1), B. Reeves Easton (1), Ray Enright (6), Lewis R. Foster (3), Peter Godfrey (2), Edmund Goulding (1), Nick Grinde (1), Alexander Hall (1), Stuart Heisler (1), H. Bruce Humberstone (1), Nathan Juran (2), William Keighley (1), James V. Kern (1), Andrew Marton (1), William McGann (1), Lothar Mendez (1), Terry Morse (1), Irving Rapper (1), Lewis Seiler (2), Vincent Sherman (1), Don Siegel (2), Noel Smith (2), A. Edward Sutherland (1), Richard Thorpe (1), Raoul Walsh (1), Sam Wood (1).

Actresses

Jane Bryan/Mrs. Justin Dart (3), Nancy Coleman (2), Bette Davis (1), Nancy Davis (1), Doris Day (3), Laraine Day (1), Olivia de Havilland (1), Rosemary De Camp (2), Angie Dickinson (2), Faye Emerson (2), Betty Field (1), Geraldine Fitzgerald (1), Rhonda Fleming (4), Bonita Granville/Mrs. Jack Wrather Jr. (1), Coleen Gray (1), Susan Hayward (2), Ruth Hussey (1), Carole Landis (2), Priscilla Lane (6), Rosemary Lane (2), Frances Langford (2), Joan Leslie (1), Viveca Lindfors (1), Anita Louise (1), Dianna Lynn (1), Dorothy Malone (1), Virginia Mayo (2), Patricia Neal (3), Gail Page (2), Eleanor Parker (2), Ginger Rogers (1), Ann Sheridan (5), Penny Singleton (2), Alexis Smith (1), Barbara Stanwyck (1), Shirley Temple (1), Rosella Towne (7), Marie Wilson (1), Jane Wyman (5).

Actors

Claude Akins (1), Eddie Albert (3), Ralph Bellamy (1), Humphrey Bogart (2), James Cagney (1), Jack Carson (2), John Cassavetes (1), Charles Coburn (2), Broderick Crawford (1), Donald Crisp (2), Robert Cummings (1), Errol Flynn (3), Preston Foster (1), Alan Hale (5), Van Heflin (1), William Hopper (6), Alan Ladd (1), Lee Marvin (1), Wayne Morris (5), George Murphy (1), Pat O'Brien (3), John Payne (1), Dick Powell (4), John Ridgely (14), Zachary Scott (1), Richard Todd (1).

Color Films

This Is The Army, It's a Great Feeling, The Last Outpost, Hong Kong, She's Working Her Way Through College, Tropic Zone, Law and Order, Cattle Queen of Montana, Tennessee's Partner, The Killers.

Studios (and number of films)

Warner Brothers (41), Universal-International (3), Paramount (3), Metro-Goldwyn-Mayer (2), R.K.O. (2), Columbia (1), NBC-TV (1).

Ronald Reagan

1950

Burns and Allen Amm-I-Dent Show (CBS)
Cast: George Burns, Gracie Allen.

The Nash Airflyte Theater (CBS) "The Case of the Missing Lady" (a.k.a. "Disappearance of Mrs. Gordon") December 7.
Producer/Director: Mark Daniels. Adapted from a story by Agatha Christie. Host: William Gaxton.
Cast: Cloris Leachman, Ian Keith, Peggy Cass.

1952

Hollywood Opening Night (NBC) "The Priceless Gift" December 29.
Producer: William Corrigan. Director: Richard Irving.

1953

The Orchid Award (ABC) (a.k.a. **The Orchid Room**)
Producers: Allen Dingwell, Harold Romm. Director: Robert Finkel.

Ford Theater (NBC) "First Born" February 5.
Cast: Nancy Davis, Nancy Guild, Tommy Rettig, Paula Corday.

Chrysler Medallion Theater (CBS) "A Job for Jimmy Valentine" July 18.
Producers: Leonard Valenta, Mort Abrams. Director: Ralph Nelson.
Cast: Dorothy Hart, Jack Arthur.

Schlitz Playhouse of Stars (CBS) "The Doctor Goes Home" July 31.
Cast: Barbara Billingsley.

B.F. Goodrich (CBS) "Burns and Allen" August 3.
Cast: George Burns, Gracie Allen.

Lux Video Theater (CBS) "Message in a Bottle" September 3.
Producer: Calvin Kuhl.
Cast: Maureen O'Sullivan.

Revlon Mirror Theater (CBS) "Next Stop Bethlehem" December 5.
Cast: Charles Bickford, Lyle Talbot.

Ford Theater (NBC) "And Suddenly You Knew" December 10.
Cast: Teresa Wright, Lee Aaker.

1954

Lux Video Theater (CBS) "A Place in the Sun" January 28.
Producer: Calvin Kuhl. Adapted from the film scenario of Theodore Dreiser's "An American Tragedy." Host: Ronald Reagan.
Cast: John Derek, Ann Blyth, Marilyn Erskine.

Schlitz Playhouse of Stars (CBS) "The Jungle Trap" February 19.
Cast: Barbara Billingsley.

Schlitz Playhouse of Stars (CBS) "The Edge of Battle" March 26.
Cast: Neville Brand.

Ford Theater (NBC) "Beneath These Waters" May 20.
Cast: John Baer.

Operation Entertainment (NBC) September 20.
Producers: Robert Welch, William Kayden. Director: William Bennington. Hosts: General Matthew B. Ridgeway, George Meany.
Cast: Tyrone Power, William Holden, Bob Hope, Danny Thomas, Danny Kaye, Edward G. Robinson, Eddie Fisher, Keenan Wynn, Pat O' Brien, Ray Bolger, Jerry Colonna, Jack Carson, Jack Haley, Debbie Reynolds, Dinah Shore, Terry Moore, Audrey Totter, Connie Haines, the Bell Sisters, Tony Romano, Patti Thomas.

General Electric Theater (CBS) "Nora" September 26.
Adapted from Henrik Ibsen's "A Doll's House."
Cast: Phyllis Thaxter, Luther Adler.

"Long Way 'Round" October 10.
Director: Don Medford. Producer: Mort Abrahams.
Cast: Nancy Davis, Nancy Gates.

"The Dark, Dark Hours" (a.k.a. "Out of the Night") December 12.
Cast: James Dean.

1955

General Electric Theater (CBS) "The Martyr" January 23.
Writer: Leo Davis. Adapted from a story by Frank O'Connor.
Cast: Brian Ahern, Lee Marvin, J.M. Kerrigan, Joseph McCallion, Noel Drayton.

"War and Peace on the Range" March 13.
Adapted from Leo Tolstoy's "War and Peace."

"Bounty Court Martial" October 9.
Writer: Elihu Winer.
Cast: Raymond Massey, Francis L. Sullivan.

"Prosper's Old Mother" November 20.
Adapted from a story by Bret Harte.
Cast: Ethel Barrymore, Charles Bronson.

"Let It Rain" December 18.
Adapted from a story by James Street.
Cast: Cloris Leachman.

1956

General Electric Theater (CBS) "Try to Remember" February 26.
Cast: Kim Hunter, Angie Dickinson, Barry Kelley.

"The Lord's Dollar" April 22.

"Fighting Professor" (a.k.a. "Professor Beware") September 30.

"The Orphans" December 2.
Cast: Kim Hunter.

The Judy Garland Show (CBS) April 8.
Producer: Sid Luft. Director: Richard Avedon.
Cast: Judy Garland, Peter Gennaro, Leonard Pennario.

1957

General Electric Theater (CBS) "No Skin Off Me" February 3.

"Bargain Bride" April 7.
Producer: William Frye. Director: Justus Addis. Writer: Jameson Brewer.
    Adapted from a story by Norma Mansfield.
Cast: Eva Bartok, Edgar Buchanan.

"A Question of Survival" May 12; repeated on **Spotlight Playhouse**, 1959.
Producer: William Frye. Director: Jules Bricken. Writer: John Dunkel.
    Adapted from a story by Floyd Beaver.
Cast: Kevin McCarthy, Robert Stevenson, Arthur Space, Dan Riss, Clark
    Howat, John War Eagle.

"Father and Son Night" October 13.
Producer: William Frye. Director: James Neilsen. Writer: William Frye.
    Adapted from his story.
Cast: Keith Larson, Bobby Clark, Jack Albertson, Joanne Davis,
    Howard McNear.

1958

General Electric Theater (CBS) "The Coward of Fort Bennett" March 16.
Cast: Neville Brand, John Dall, Jason Robards Sr., Raymond Greenleaf,
    Herbert Anderson, Robert Simon, Arthur Space.

"No Hiding Place" April 6.
Producer: William Frye. Director: Andrew McCullough. Writer: Kathleen Hite.
    Adapted from a story by Beth Day.
Cast: Geraldine Page, David Opathashu, Pernell Roberts, Whit Bissell, Amy
    Douglas, Gavin MacLeod, Jean Engstrom.

"The Castaway" October 12.
Adapted from a story by Guy de Maupassant.
Cast: Robert Fuller, Jim Davis, Jennifer West, Harold Stone, Ethel Shutta,
    Michael Rye.

"A Turkey for the President" November 23.
Cast: Nancy Davis, Ward Bond, Tommy Nolan, Joanne Davis, Warren Wade,
    Charles Seel.

1959

General Electric Theater (CBS) "Deed of Mercy" March 1.
Producer: William Frye. Director: James Neilsen. Writer: John McGreevey.
    Adapted from a story by Philip MacDonald.
Cast: Carol Lynley, Agnes Moorehead, Cecil Smith, Jeanne Bates, Mike
    Ragan, Carl Esmond, John Beradino.

"Nobody's Child" May 10.
Producer: William Frye. Director: Robert Sinclair. Writer: Ben Canfield.
Cast: Diane Brewster, Evelyn Rudie, Sheilah Graham, Jean Carson, Steve
    Mitchell, Charity Grace, Nolan Leary, Selmer Jackson, Maggie McCarter.

"Signs of Love" November 8.
Cast: Paula Raymond, Pat Carroll, Francis X. Bushman, Francis Robinson,
    Bess Flowers, Howard McNear, George Neise, James Logan.

"The House of Truth" December 13.
Cast: Phyllis Thaxter, Alice Backes, Linda Hong, Dick Kay Hong, Phillip Ahn,
    Guy Lee, Allen Jung.

1960

General Electric Theater (CBS) "So Deadly, So Evil" March 13.
Producer: Joe Naar. Director: Don Weis. Writer: Jerry Sohl. Adapted from a story by Holly Roth.
Cast: Peggy Lee, Gavin MacLeod, Robert Hopkins, Terry Loomis, Michael Granger, Les Green.

"Goodbye, My Love" October 16.
Producer: Stanley Rubin. Director: Ida Lupino. Writer: Sidney Carroll.
Cast: Anne Baxter, Chester Stratton, Nestor Paiva, Howard Wendell, Del Moore, Alan Reynolds, Angela Stevens, Ralph Sanford, Mary Brenman.

"Learn To Say Goodbye" December 4.
Producer: Stanley Rubin. Director: Ida Lupino. Writer: Stirling Silliphant. Adapted from a story by Jessamyn West.
Cast: Coleen Gray, Frank Wilcox, Michael Burns, Claire Carleton, Bud Osborne, Wally Brown, John McKee, Roy Rowan, Frank Cady, George Barrows.

The June Allyson Show for DuPont (CBS) "The Way Home" January 18.
Producer: Dick Powell.
Cast: Eugenie Leontovich.

The Swingin' Years (NBC) February 9.
Producers: Hubbell Robinson, Gil Rodin. Director: Barry Shear. Host of variety musical special.
Cast: Gene Krupa, Count Basie, Anita O'Day, Guy Lombardo, Helen O'Connell.

The Swingin' Years (NBC) March 8.
Producers: Hubbell Robinson, Gil Rodin. Director: Barry Shear. Host of musical variety special.
Cast: Jo Stafford, Woody Herman, Vaughn Monroe, Eddie Howard, Dinah Washington, Jack Fina.

1961

General Electric Theater (CBS) "The Devil You Say" January 22.
Producer: Stanley Rubin. Director: Richard Irving. Writer: Jameson Brewer. Adapted from a story by Ira Levin.
Cast: Sid Caesar, Patricia Barry, George Conrad, Ken Hooker.

"The Iron Silence" September 24.
Director: Ida Lupino. Writer: Ken Kolb. Adapted from a story by Guy de Maupassant.
Cast: Carol Lawrence, Vic Morrow, Abraham Sofaer, James Westerfield, Gloria Marshall, Elisa Palfi, Nina Bara, Stan Kahn, Peter Walker, Rosalind Saunders.

"Money and the Minister" November 26; repeated July 1, 1962.
Writer: Charlotte Armstrong. Adapted from her story.
Cast: Nancy Davis, Gary Merrill, Fay Wray, Jaye P. Morgan, Connie Gilchrist, Ellen Corby, Richard Hale, Lillian Bronson, Robert Cornthwaite.

Dick Powell's Zane Grey Theater (CBS) "The Long Shadow" January 19.
Producers: Aaron Spelling, Hal Hudson. Director: Budd Boetticher. Writer: Richard Fielder. Host: Dick Powell.
Cast: Nancy Davis, Scott Marlowe, Roberta Shore, Walter Sande, John Pickard, Bill Brauer.

The Bob Hope Show (NBC) February 15.
Cast: Dana Andrews, Lucille Ball, Julie London, Jayne Mansfield, Dean Martin, Ginger Rogers, Jane Russell, Tuesday Weld, Jane Wyman.

The Dick Powell Show (NBC) "Amos Burke: Who Killed Julie Greer?" September 26.
Producer: Aaron Spelling. Director: Robert Ellis Miller. Writer: Frank D. Gilroy.
Cast: Dick Powell, Mickey Rooney, Lloyd Bridges, Jack Carson, Edgar Bergen, Carolyn Jones, Kay Thompson, Dean Jones, Nick Adams, Ralph Bellamy.

1962

General Electric Theater (CBS) "The Wall Between" January 7.
Producer: Stanley Rubin. Director: Harry Keller. Writer: Alvin Boretz.
Cast: Stephen Boyd, Gloria Talbott, Everett Sloane, Walter Sande, Maxine Stewart, Jennifer Gillespie, Stephanie Hill, Jess Kirkpatrick.

"Shadow of a Hero" February 4.
Producer: Stanley Rubin. Director: Herschell Daugherty. Writer: Robert Dozier. Adapted from a story by William Clotworthy.
Cast: David Janssen, Charles Robinson, Arlene Whelan, Nelson Olmsted, Marianna Case, Harvey Stephens, Olan Soule, John Mauldin, Tom Franklin, John Jacobs.

"I Was a Spy" March 18.
Producer: Ronald Reagan. Director: Charles Haas.
Cast: Jeanne Crain, Lance Fuller.

"My Dark Days — Prelude" August 19.
Producer: Ronald Reagan. Director: Charles Haas.
Cast: Jeanne Crain, Lance Fuller, Patricia Huston, Robert Emhardt, Patrick McVey, Susan Gordon, Carl Benton.

"My Dark Days — Aftermath" August 26.
Producer: Ronald Reagan. Director: Charles Haas.
Cast: Jeanne Crain, Lance Fuller, Patricia Huston, Robert Emhardt, Patrick McVey, Susan Gordon, Carl Benton.

1963
Wagon Train (ABC) "The Fort Pierce Story" September 23.
Cast: Ann Blyth, John Doucette, Kathie Browne.

1964
Kraft Suspense Theater (ABC) "A Cruel and Unusual Night" June 4.
Cast: Scott Marlowe, Anne Helm.

News Special — "A Time for Choosing" October 27. Speech for Senator Barry Goldwater, Republican Candidate for President.

Death Valley Days "Tribute to the Dog" December 27.
Cast: Carter Johnson, Danny Flower, Ralph Moody.

1965
Death Valley Days "The Battle of San Francisco Bay" March 18.

"Raid on the San Francisco Mint" March 10.
Cast: Judson Pratt, Vaughn Taylor, John Clarke.

"Temporary Warden" September 30.
Cast: Rudolfo Acosta, Jim Bannon, George Mudock.

"No Place for a Lady" October 21.
Cast: Linda Marsh, Simon Scott, Maidie Norman.

"A City Is Born" October 22.
Cast: June Lockhart, Tod Hunter, Oscar Beregi, Jack Lambert.

1967
The Joey Bishop Show (ABC)
Host: Joey Bishop. Announcer: Regis Philbin.

1968
CBS Reports — News Special (CBS) "What About Ronald Reagan?"

1975
Dean's Place (NBC) September 6.
Producer/Director: Greg Garrison.
Cast: Dean Martin, Nancy Reagan, Angie Dickinson, Robert Mitchum, Peter Graves, Jack Cassidy, Vincent Gardenia.

1981
Bob Hope Special: Bob Hope Presents a Celebration with Stars of Comedy and Music (NBC) October 22.
Cast: Nancy Reagan, Pearl Bailey, Debby Boone, Foster Brooks, Glen Campbell, Sammy Davis Jr., Gordon MacRae, Tony Orlando, Mark Russell, Danny Thomas, Walter Annenberg, George Bush, Margaret Truman, Gerald R. Ford, Alexander Haig, Henry Kissinger, Thomas 'Tip' O'Neill, Pierre Trudeau, Casper Weinberger.

1982
Roy Acuff — 50 Years the King of Country Music (NBC) March 1.
Producers: Joseph Cates, Chet Hagan. Director: Walter C. Miller.
Hostess: Minnie Pearl. Special Guest: Roy Acuff.
Cast: Eddy Arnold, Chet Atkins, Gene Autry, Crystal Gayle, Larry Gatlin, Emmylou Harris, Barbara Mandrell, Dolly Parton, Kenny Rogers, Hank Williams Jr., Ernest Tubb, Don Gibson, Bill Anderson.

Christmas in Washington (NBC) December 13.
Executive Producer: George Stevens Jr.
Cast: Nancy Reagan, Dinah Shore, Diahann Carol, Ben Vereen, Barbara Mandrell, John Schneider, the Shiloh Baptist Church Choir.

1983
Bob Hope Special: Happy Birthday, Bob! (NBC) May 23.
Cast: Nancy Reagan, Brooke Shields, Cheryl Tiegs, Christie Brinkley, Dolores Hope, Lucille Ball, George Burns, Lynda Carter, Kathryn Crosby, Phyllis Diller, Ann Jillian, Loretta Lynn, Barbara Mandrell, Dudley Moore, George C. Scott, Tom Selleck, Flip Wilson.

1984
Christmas in Washington (NBC) December 16.
Executive Producer: George Stevens Jr.
Cast: Nancy Reagan, the Osmond Brothers, Marie Osmond, Donny Osmond, Roger Mudd, Nell Carter, Frederica VonStade.

F I L M O G R A P H Y

Nancy Davis

1949

The Doctor and the Girl (a.k.a. **Bodies and Souls**). Metro-Goldwyn-Mayer.
Director: Curtis Bernhardt. Writer: Theodore Reeves. Producer: Pandro S. Berman.
Cast: Glenn Ford, Charles Coburn, Gloria DeHaven, Janet Leigh, Bruce Bennett, Warner Anderson, Arthur Franz.

East Side, West Side. Metro-Goldwyn-Mayer.
Director: Mervyn LeRoy. Writer: Isobel Lennart. Producer: Voldemar Vetloguin.
Cast: Barbara Stanwyck, James Mason, Van Heflin, Ava Gardner, Cyd Charisse, Gale Sondergaard, William Conrad, Beverly Michaels, William Frawley, Tom Powers.

1950

Shadow on the Wall (a.k.a. **Death in a Doll's House**). Metro-Goldwyn-Mayer. Completed in 1949.
Director: Patrick Jackson. Writer: William Ludwig. Producer: Robert Sisk.
Cast: Ann Southern, Zachary Scott, Gigi Perreau, Kristine Miller, Barbara Billingsley.

The Next Voice You Hear. . . . Metro-Goldwyn-Mayer.
Director: William A. Wellman. Writer: Charles Schnee. Producer: Dore Schary.
Cast: James Whitmore, Gary Gray, Lillian Bronson, Jeff Corey.

1951

Night Into Morning (a.k.a. **People We Love**). Metro-Goldwyn-Mayer.
Director: Fletcher Markle. Writers: Karl Tunberg, Leonard Spigelgass. Producer: Edward H. Knopf.
Cast: Ray Milland, John Hodiak, Lewis Stone, Jean Hagen, Rosemary De Camp, Dawn Addams.

1952

It's a Big Country. Metro-Goldwyn-Mayer. ("Four Eyes," one of seven episodes)
Director: Don Hartman. Writer: George Wells. Producer: Robert Sisk. Other Directors: Clarence Brown, John Sturges, Richard Thorpe, Charles Vidor, William A. Wellman, Don Weis.
Cast: Frederic March, Angela Clarke, Bobby Hyatt. Other Actors: Ethel Barrymore, Keefe Brasselle, Gary Cooper, Van Johnson, Gene Kelly, Janet Leigh, Marjorie Main, George Murphy, William Powell, S.Z. Sakall, Lewis Stone, James Whitmore, Keenan Wynn, Leon Ames.

Shadow in the Sky (a.k.a. **Rain, Rain, Go Away**). Metro-Goldwyn-Mayer.
Director: Fred M. Wilcox. Writer: Ben Maddow. Producer: William H. Wright.
Cast: Ralph Meeker, James Whitmore, Jean Hagen, Eduard Franz, John Lupton.

Talk About a Stranger. Metro-Goldwyn-Mayer.
Director: David Bradley. Writer: Margaret Fitts. Producer: Richard Goldstone.
Cast: George Murphy, Billy Gray, Lewis Stone, Kurt Kasznar.

1953

Donovan's Brain. United Artists.
Director/Writer: Felix Feist. Producer: Tom Gries.
Cast: Lew Ayres, Gene Evans, Steve Brodie, Tom Powers.

Remake of The Lady and the Monster (a.k.a. The Monster and the Lady; rereleased as Tiger Man) (1944). Republic Pictures.
Director: George Sherman. Based on the novel by Curt Siodmak.
Cast: Vera Hruba Ralston, Richard Arlen, Erich von Stroheim, Sidney Blackmer, Helen Vinson, Mary Nash, Lola Montez.

Remade as The Brain (a.k.a. Vengeance; A Dead Man Seeks His Murderer) (1962). Governor Films.
Director: Freddie Francis.
Cast: Peter Van Eyck, Anne Heywood, Cecil Parker, Bernard Lee, Frank Forsyth, Jack McGowran.

1957

Hellcats of the Navy. Columbia.
Director: Nathan Juran. Writers: David Lang, Raymond Marcus. Producer: Charles H. Schneer.
Cast: Ronald Reagan, Arthur Franz, Robert Arthur, William Leslie.

1958

Crash Landing (a.k.a. Rescue at Sea; The Dark Wave). Columbia. Completed in 1955.
Director: Fred F. Sears. Writer: Fred Freiberger. Producer: Sam Katzman.
Cast: Gary Merrill, Irene Hervey, Roger Smith, Bek Nelson, Jewell Lain.

Nancy Davis

1949

The Philco Television Playhouse (NBC) ''Ramshackle Inn'' January 2.
Producer: Fred Coe. Adapted from the play by George Batson. Host: Bert Lytell.
Cast: ZaSu Pitts, Joe Downing, Robert Tome.

1953

Schlitz Playhouse of Stars (CBS) ''Twenty-two Sycamore Road'' June 5.
Cast: Willard Parker.

Ford Theater (NBC) ''First Born'' February 5.
Cast: Ronald Reagan, Nancy Guild, Tommy Rettig, Paula Corday.

1954

Schlitz Playhouse of Stars (CBS) ''The Pearl Street Incident'' May 14.
Cast: Horace MacMahon, Jacqueline de Witt.

General Electric Theater (CBS) ''Long Way 'Round'' October 10.
Producer: Mort Abrahams. Director: Don Medford.
Cast: Ronald Reagan, Nancy Gates.

1955

Climax! (CBS) ''Bail out at 43,000'' December 29.
Writer: Paul Monash.
Cast: Charlton Heston, Lee Marvin, Richard Boone.
Basis of 1957 United Artists film directed by Francis D. Lyon.
Cast: John Payne, Karen Steel, Paul Kelly, Richard Eyer.

1956

General Electric Theater (CBS) ''That's the Man!'' April 15.
Adapted from a story by Melville Davison Post.
Cast: Ray Milland.

1958

General Electric Theater (CBS) ''A Turkey for the President'' November 23.
Cast: Ronald Reagan, Ward Bond, Tommy Nolan, Joanne Davis, Warren
   Wade, Charles Seel.

1960

General Electric Theater (CBS) ''The Playoff'' November 20.
Director: James Neilson. Writer: Robert Dozier.
Cast: Dana Andrews, Ryan O'Neal, Regis Toomey, Denny Miller, Carl Bentor
   Reid, Vin Scully.

1961

Dick Powell's Zane Grey Theater (CBS) ''The Long Shadow'' January 19.
Producers: Aaron Spelling, Hal Hudson. Director: Budd Boetticher. Writer:
   Richard Fielder. Host: Dick Powell.
Cast: Ronald Reagan, Scott Marlowe, Roberta Shore, Walter Sande, John
   Pickard, Bill Brauer.

Tall Man (NBC) ''Shadow of the Past'' October 7.
Cast: Charles Aidman, Barbara Perkins.

General Electric Theater (CBS) ''Money and the Minister'' November 26.
Writer: Charlotte Armstrong.
Cast: Ronald Reagan, Gary Merrill, Fay Wray, Jaye P. Morgan, Connie
   Gilchrist, Ellen Corby, Richard Hale, Lillian Bronson, Robert Cornthwaite.

1962

The Dick Powell Theater (NBC) ''Obituary for Mr. X'' January 23.
Cast: Gary Merrill, Steve Cochran, John Ireland, Dina Merrill.

87th Precinct (NBC) ''King's Ransom'' February 19.
Cast: Charles Aidman, Charles McGraw, Dan Tobin.

Wagon Train (ABC) ''The Sam Darland Story'' December 26.
Cast: Art Linkletter.

1975

Dean's Place (NBC) September 6.
Producer/Director: Greg Garrison.
Cast: Dean Martin, Ronald Reagan, Angie Dickinson, Robert Mitchum, Peter
   Graves, Jack Cassidy, Vincent Gardenia.

1981

Bob Hope Special: Bob Hope Presents a Celebration with Stars of
  Comedy and Music (NBC) October 22.

Cast: Ronald Reagan, Pearl Bailey, Debby Boone, Foster Brooks, Glen
  Campbell, Sammy Davis Jr., Gordon MacRae, Tony Orlando, Mark Russell,
  Danny Thomas, Walter Annenberg, George Bush, Margaret Truman,
  Gerald R. Ford, Alexander Haig, Henry Kissinger, Thomas 'Tip' O'Neill,
  Pierre Trudeau, Casper Weinberger.

1982

Christmas in Washington (NBC) December 13.

Executive Producer: George Stevens Jr.

Cast: Ronald Reagan, Dinah Shore, Diahann Carol, Ben Vereen, Barbara
  Mandrell, John Schneider, the Shiloh Baptist Church Choir.

1983

Diff'rent Strokes (NBC) March 19.

Cast: Gary Coleman, Todd Bridges, Conrad Bain, Dana Plato.

Bob Hope Special: Happy Birthday, Bob! (NBC) May 23.

Cast: Ronald Reagan, Brooke Shields, Cheryl Tiegs, Christie Brinkley, Dolores
  Hope, Lucille Ball, George Burns, Lynda Carter, Kathryn Crosby, Phyllis
  Diller, Ann Jillian, Loretta Lynn, Barbara Mandrell, Dudley Moore, George
  C. Scott, Tom Selleck, Flip Wilson.

The Chemical People (PBS) November 2.

1984

Christmas in Washington (NBC) December 16.

Executive Producer: George Stevens Jr.

Cast: Ronald Reagan, the Osmond Brothers, Marie Osmond, Donny
  Osmond, Roger Mudd, Nell Carter, Frederica VonStade.

Stage Credits

1944

Ramshackle Inn — Shubert Theater, Detroit, Michigan.

1946

Lute Song — Plymouth Theater, New York.

Cordelia — Shubert Theater, New Haven, Connecticut.

1947

The Late Christopher Bean — Civic Theater, Chicago, Illinois.

Ronald Reagan — Film Posters

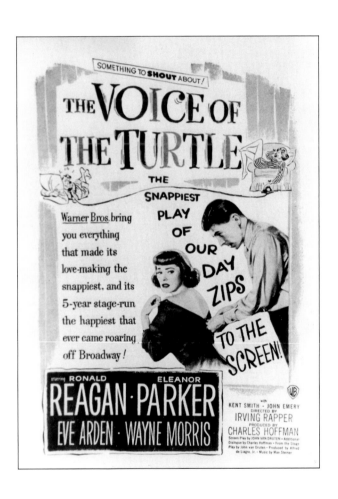

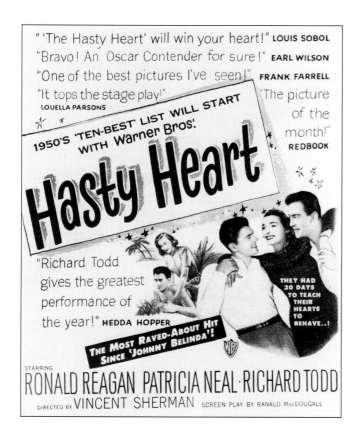

124

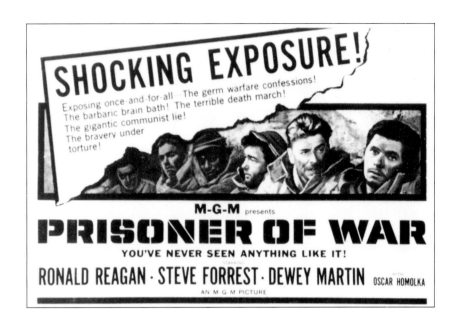

Ever See These Three Before?

Name of Joe Smith and family. Joe's an aircraft worker. Good one, too. Loves his wife. Bowls with the boys every Wednesday…Mary runs the house. Sticks to the budget. Saves boxtops for a set of dishes. Makes meatloaf for Tuesday supper… Johnny, their son. Hates meatloaf. Hates math too. Works at his paper route so he can get that shiny new bike…Ordinary folks… average Americans. But one night at eight-thirty they heard a strange voice on the radio… How their lives were changed is the story of this picture.

M·G·M *presents a Wonderful Picture*

the next voice you hear…

JAMES WHITMORE • NANCY DAVIS

Written by CHARLES SCHNEE

Suggested by a story by GEORGE SUMNER ALBEE

Directed by WILLIAM A. WELLMAN

Produced by DORE SCHARY

A METRO-GOLDWYN-MAYER PICTURE

This Political Scandal Must Be Investigated!

54% of people with AIDS in NYC are Black or Hispanic... AIDS is the No. 1 killer of women between the ages of 24 and 29 in NYC...
By 1991, more people will have died of AIDS than in the *entire* Vietnam War... What is Reagan's *real* policy on AIDS?
Genocide of all Non-whites, Non-males, and Non-heterosexuals?...
SILENCE = DEATH

BIBLIOGRAPHY

Visual Bibliography

This listing contains books which have visual reproductions of Ronald and Nancy Reagan in paintings, sculpture, drawings, prints and photographs.

Adler, Bill. *Ronnie and Nancy – A Very Special Love Story.* New York: Crown Pub., Inc., 1985.

Allyson, June with Leighton, Frances Spatz. *June Allyson.* New York: G.P. Putnam's Sons, 1982.

Amalgamated Press, Ltd., eds. *Picture Show Annual, 1948, 1950.* London: Fleetway House.

Anderson, Janice. *Ronald Reagan.* New York: Exeter Books, 1982.

Anderson, Martin. *Revolution.* San Diego: Harcourt, Brace, Jovanovich, 1988.

Anger, Kenneth. *Hollywood Babylon II.* New York: Plume/New American Library, 1984.

Appel, Alfred Jr. *Signs of Life.* New York: Alfred A. Knopf, 1983.

Ashbery, John, Cutler, Jane and Stein, Judith. *Red Grooms – A Retrospective 1956-1984.* Philadelphia: Pennsylvania Academy of the Fine Arts, 1985.

Auth, Tony. *Lost in Space – The Reagan Years.* Kansas City, MO: Andrews and McMeel, 1988.

Aylesworth, Thomas G. *The Best of Warner Bros.* New York: Gallery Books, 1986.

Baker, Howard. *Howard Baker's Washington.* New York: W.W. Norton and Co., 1982.

Barnet, Richard J. *The Alliance – America Europe Japan.* New York: Simon and Schuster, 1983.

Barris, Alex. *Hollywood's Other Men.* South Brunswick, NJ: A.S. Barnes, 1975.
— *Stop the Presses! The Newspaper in American Films.* South Brunswick, NJ: A.S. Barnes, 1976.

Bartvedt, Alf, Eirheim, Jeanne, and Meyrick, John. *Insight – Aspects of British and American Civilization.* Fagernes: Aschehoug, 1986.

Basinger, Jeanine. *Shirley Temple.* New York: Pyramid, 1975.

Bego, Mark, ed. *The Best of Modern Screen.* New York: St. Martin's Press, 1986.

Behlmer, Rudy. *Inside Warner Bros. (1935-1951)* New York: Viking Penguin, Inc., 1985.

Bell, Terrel H. *The Thirteenth Man – A Reagan Cabinet Memoir.* New York: The Free Press, 1988.

Benedict, Brad. *Fame – Portraits of Celebrated People.* New York: Harmony Books, 1980.
— *Fame 2 – Portraits and Pop Culture.* New York: Indigo Books, 1984.

Bergan, Ronald. *Sports in the Movies.* London: Proteus Publishing Co., Inc., 1982.
— *The United Artists Story.* New York: Crown Publishers, Inc., 1986.

Blassingame, Wyatt. *The Look-It-Up Book of Presidents.* New York: Random House, 1984.

Block, Herb. *Herblock Through the Looking Glass.* New York: W.W. Norton and Co., 1984.

Blum, Daniel. *A Pictorial History of the Talkies.* New York: G.P. Putnam's Sons, 1958.
— *Screen World, 1949, 1951, 1952, 1953, 1954, 1955, 1956, 1958.* New York: Greenberg.

Bogdanovich, Peter. *Allan Dwan – The Last Pioneer.* New York: Praeger, 1971.

Borland, Jan and Vance, Malcolm. *The Ronald Reagan Hollywood Quiz Book.* New York: Exeter Books, 1981.
— *Ronald Reagan Political Quiz Book.* New York: Exeter Books, 1981.

Boyarsky, Bill. *The Rise of Ronald Reagan.* New York: Random House, 1968.

Bradlee, Ben Jr. *Guts and Glory – The Rise and Fall of Oliver North.* New York: Donald I. Fine, Inc., 1988.

Brockman, Alfred. *The Movie Book – The 1930s.* New York: Crescent Books, 1987.

Brode, Douglas. *Lost Films of the Fifties.* Secaucus, NJ: The Citadel Press, 1988.

Brown, Jay A. *Rating the Movies*. New York: Beekman House, 1982.

Bull, Clarence Sinclair and Lee, Raymond. *The Faces of Hollywood*. South Brunswick, NJ: A.S. Barnes, 1968.

Burchill, Julie. *Girls on Film*. New York: Pantheon Books, 1986.

Burns, George. *Dr. Burns' Prescription for Happiness*. New York: Perigee, 1984.
— *Gracie A Love Story*. New York: G.P. Putnam's Sons, 1988.

Burson, Nancy with Ewing, William A. and McDermott, Jeanne. *Composites – Computer-Generated Portraits*. New York: Beech Tree Books/William Morrow, 1986.

Cameron, Ian. *A Pictorial History of Crime Films*. London: Hamlyn, 1975.

Cannon, Lou. *Reagan*. New York: G.P. Putnam's Sons, 1982.

Carlinsky, Dan. *Celebrity Yearbook*. Los Angeles: Price/Stern/Sloan Pub., Inc., 1983.

Caroli, Betty Boyd. *First Ladies*. New York: Oxford University Press, 1987.

Carr, Larry. *More Fabulous Faces*. Garden City, NY: Doubleday and Co., Inc., 1979.

Carter, Jimmy. *Keeping Faith – Memoirs of a President*. New York: Bantam Books, 1982.

Charren, Peggy and Sandler, Martin W. *Changing Channels*. Reading, MA: Addison-Wesley Pub. Co., 1983.

Cocchi, John. *The Westerns – A Picture Quiz Book*. New York: Dover Pub., Inc., 1976.

Cohen, Daniel and Susan. *Encyclopedia of Movie Stars*. New York: Gallery Books, 1985.

Cohen, William S. and Mitchell, George J. *Men of Zeal*. New York: Viking, 1988.

Conrad, Paul. *Drawn and Quartered*. New York: Harry N. Abrams, Inc., 1985.

Cook, Pam, ed. *The Cinema Book*. London: British Film Institute, 1985.

Crawley, Tony. *Screen Dreams – The Hollywood Pinup*. New York: Delilah/Putnam, 1982.

Cross, Robin. *The Big Book of B Movies or How Low Was My Budget*. New York: St. Martin's Press, 1981.
— *2000 Movies: the 1940s*. New York: Arlington House, 1985.
— *The Big Book of British Films*. London: Sidgwick and Jackson, 1984.

Cunliffe, Marcus. *The Presidency*. Boston: Houghton Mifflin Co., 1987.

D'Agostino, Peter and Montadas, Antonio, eds. *The Unnecessary Image*. New York: Tanam Press, 1982.

Dallinger, Nat. *Unforgettable Hollywood*. New York: William Morrow and Co., Inc., 1982.

Dalton, David. *James Dean – American Icon*. New York: St. Martin's Press, 1984.

Danzinger, James, ed., Capa, Cornell, foreword. *Visual Aid*. New York: Pantheon Books, 1986.

David, Lester and David, Irene. *The Shirley Temple Story*. New York: G.P. Putnam's Sons, 1983.

Davis, Bette with Herskowitz, Michael. *This 'N' That*. New York: G.P. Putnam's Sons, 1987.

Deaver, Michael K. with Herskowitz, Mickey. *Behind the Scenes*. New York: William Morrow and Co., 1987.

DeGregorio, William A. *The Complete Book of United States Presidents*. New York: Dembner Books, 1984.

DeMause, Lloyd. *Reagan's America*. New York: Creative Roots, Inc., 1984.

Dickens, Homer. *The Films of Ginger Rogers*. Secaucus, NJ: The Citadel Press, 1975.

Donaldson, Sam. *Hold On, Mr. President!* New York: Fawcett Crest, 1988.

Douglas, Kirk. *The Ragman's Son – An Autobiography*. New York: Simon and Schuster, 1988.

Druxman, Michael B. *One Good Film Deserves Another*. South Brunswick, NJ: A.S. Barnes, 1977.

Dunean, David Douglas. *Self-Portrait: U.S.A.* New York: Harry N. Abrams, Inc., 1969.

Eames, John Douglas. *The MGM Story.* New York: Crown Publishers, Inc., 1975.
— *The Paramount Story.* New York: Crown Publishers, Inc., 1985.

Edwards, Anne. *Early Reagan.* New York: William Morrow and Co., 1987.

Eisenstaedt, Alfred with Kunhardt, Philip B., Jr. *Eisenstaedt's Album.* NY: Viking Press, 1976.

Elterman, Brad. *Shoot the Stars.* Beverly Hills: California Features International, Inc., 1985.

Elwood, Roger. *Nancy Reagan: A Special Kind of Love.* New York: Pocket Books, 1976.

Essoe, Gabe. *The Book of TV Lists.* Westport, CT: Arlington House, 1981.

Evans, Michael with Will, George F., Livingston, Jane, Fern, Alan. *People and Power - Portraits from the Federal Village.* New York: Harry N. Abrams, Inc., 1985.

Fehrenbacher, Don E. and Tutorow, Norman E. *California - An Illustrated History.* New York: Van Nostrand, 1968.

Feiffer, Jules. *Ronald Reagan in Movie America.* Kansas City, MO: Andrews and McMeel, 1988.

Feldman, Frayda and Schellmann, Jorg, eds. *Andy Warhol Prints.* New York: Abbeville Press, 1985.

Finch, Christopher and Rosenkrantz. *Gone Hollywood.* Garden City, NY: Doubleday and Co., Inc., 1979.

Fireman, Judy, ed. *TV Book.* New York: Workman Pub. Co., 1977.

Fitzgerald, Jim and Boswell, John. *First Family Paper Doll and Cut-out Book.* New York: Dell, 1981.

Fitzgerald, Michael G. *Universal Pictures.* New Rochelle, NY: Arlington House, 1977.

Ford, Gerald R. *A Time To Heal - Autobiography.* New York: Harper and Row, Pub., 1979.

Frank, Alan. *Sinatra.* New York: Leon Amiel, 1978.

Fraser, George MacDonald. *The Hollywood History of the World.* New York: Beech Tree Books/William Morrow, 1988.

Fresco, Monty. *Photographs Are My Life.* New York: Arco Pub. Co., 1983.

Friedman, Stanley P. *Ronald Reagan.* New York: Dodd, Mead and Co., 1986.

Galbraith, Evan G. *Ambassador in Paris.* Washington, DC: Regnery Gateway, 1987.

Gardner, Gerald. *The Actor - A Photographic Interview with Ronald Reagan.* New York: Pocket Books, 1981.
— *Who's in Charge Here? Campaign Edition.* New York: Ballantine Books, 1980.
— *Who's in Charge Here? 1988.* New York: Bantam Books, 1988.

Gelb, Alan. *The Doris Day Scrapbook.* New York: Grosset and Dunlap, Inc., 1977.

Giannetti, Louis. *Flashback - A Brief History of Film.* Englewood Cliffs, NJ: Prentice Hall, 1986.

Goldman, Peter and Fuller, Tony. *The Quest for the Presidency 1984.* New York: Bantam Books, 1985.

Goldstein, Norm. *Frank Sinatra - Ol' Blue Eyes.* New York: Holt, Rinehart, Winston, 1982.

Goldwater, Barry M. with Casserly, Jack. *Goldwater.* New York: Doubleday, 1988.

Graham, Ellen. *The Growling Gourmet.* New York: Simon and Schuster, 1976.

Graham, Sheilah. *Hollywood Revisited.* New York: St. Martin's Press, 1985.

Green, Mark and MacColl, Gail. *There He Goes Again: Ronald Reagan's Reign of Error.* New York: Pantheon Books, 1983.

Grey, Edward. *Presidents of the United States.* New York: Gallery Books, 1988.

Gurney, Gene. *Kingdoms of Europe.* New York: Crown Pub., Inc., 1982.

Gutstein, Linda. *History of Jews in America.* Secaucus, NJ: Chart Well Books, 1988.

Haig, Alexander M. *Caveat - Realism and Foreign Policy.* New York: Macmillan, 1984.

Halsman, Phillipe. *Portraits.* New York: McGraw-Hill Book Co., 1983.

Hammer, Armand with Lyndon, Neil. *Hammer.* New York: G.P. Putnam's Sons, 1987.

Harris, Kenneth. *Thatcher.* Boston: Little, Brown and Co., 1988.

Hartman, Geoffrey H., ed. *Bitburg in Moral and Political Perspective.* Bloomington: Indiana University Press, 1986.

Harwood, Richard, ed. *The Pursuit of the Presidency 1980.* New York: Berkley Books, Washington Post, 1980.

Healy, Diana Dixon. *America's First Ladies.* New York: Atheneum, 1988.

Heinonen, Kai. *Let's Fact It!* New York: Phaedra, Inc., 1971.

Hewitt, Don. *Minute By Minute. . .* New York: Random House, 1985.

Higham, Charles. *Bette – The Life of Bette Davis.* New York: Macmillan, 1981.
— *Warner Brothers.* New York: Charles Scribner's Sons, 1975.

Hirschhorn, Clive. *The Universal Story.* New York: Crown Publishers, Inc., 1983.
— *The Warner Bros. Story.* New York: Crown Publishers, Inc., 1979.

Hirschhorn, Joel. *Rating the Movie Stars.* New York: Beekman House, 1983.

Hofmekler, Ori. *Hofmekler's Gallery.* New York: Times Books, 1987.

Hotchner, A.E. *Doris Day – Her Own Story.* New York: William Morrow and Co., Inc., 1976.

Hudson, Rock and Davidson, Sara. *Rock Hudson – His Story.* New York: William Morrow and Co., Inc., 1986.

Hyams, Joe. *War Movies.* New York: Gallery Books, 1984.

Iacocca, Lee and Kleinfield, Sonny. *Talking Straight.* Toronto: Bantam Books, 1988.

Jamieson, Kathleen Hall and Birdsell, David S. *Presidential Debates.* New York: Oxford, 1988.

Jewell, Derek. *Frank Sinatra.* Boston: Little, Brown and Co., 1985.

Jewell, Richard B. with Harbin, Vernon. *The RKO Story.* New York: Arlington House, 1982.

Jones, Ken D. and McClure, Arthur F. *Hollywood at War.* New York: Castle Books, 1973.

Judis, John B. *William F. Buckley, Jr. Patron Saint of the Conservatives.* New York: Simon and Schuster, 1988.

Karney, Robyn, ed. *The Movie Stars Story.* New York: Crescent Books, 1986.

Kass, Judith M. *Olivia deHavilland.* New York: Pyramid, 1976.

Keaton, Diane and Heiferman, Marvin, eds. *Still Life.* New York: Simon and Schuster, 1983.

Kelley, Kitty. *Elizabeth Taylor – The Last Star.* New York: Simon and Schuster, 1981.

Kelly, Sean. *Spitting Images.* San Diego: Harcourt, Brace, Jovanovich, 1987.

Knight, Arthur, introduction. *The New York Times Directory of the Film.* New York: Arno Press / Random House, 1971.

Koppes, Clayton R. and Black, Gregory D. *Hollywood Goes to War.* New York: The Free Press, 1987.

Krause, Emil. *Bonzo Goes to Washington.* South Bend, IN: and books, 1980.

LaGuardia, Robert and Arceri, Gene. *Red – The Tempestuous Life of Susan Hayward.* New York: Macmillan, 1985.

Lawrence, Sidney and Yau, John. *Roger Brown.* New York: George Braziller, 1987.

Leamer, Laurence. *Make-Believe – The Story of Nancy and Ronald Reagan.* New York: Harper and Row, 1983.

Ledeen, Michael A. *Perilous Stagecraft.* New York: Charles Scribner's Sons, 1988.

Leighton, Frances Spratz. *The Search for the Real Nancy Reagan.* New York: Macmillan, 1987.

LeRoy, Mervyn with Kleiner, Dick. *Mervyn LeRoy: Take One.* New York: Hawthorn Books, 1974.

Levesque, G. Victor and Zuker, Irwin. *Re-run with Ronnie.* Hollywood: Zadco, 1966.

Libby, Bill. *They Didn't Win the Oscars.* Westport, CT: Arlington House, 1980.

Lindfors, Viveca. *Viveka. . .Viveka.* New York: Everest House, 1981.

Linet, Beverly. *Portrait of a Survivor – Susan Hayward.* New York: Berkley Books, 1981.

Lloyd, Ann and Robinson, David, eds. *They Went That-A-Way.* London: Orbis Publishing, 1982.

137

Loengard, John. *Life Classic Photographers.* Waltham, MA: New York Graphic Society / Little, Brown and Co., 1988.

Maloney, William E. *President Ronnie.* New York: Perigee Books, 1981.

Maltin, Leonard, ed. *Hollywood the Movie Factory.* New York: Popular Library, 1976.

Matilsky, Barbara C. *Classical Myth and Imagery in Contemporary Art.* Flushing, NY: The Queen's Museum, 1988.

Mauldin, Bill. *Let's Declare Ourselves Winners. . . and Get the Hell Out.* Novato, CA: Presidio Press, 1985.

Mayer, Jan and McManus, Doyle. *Landslide – The Unmaking of the President, 1984-1988.* Boston: Houghton Mifflin Co., 1988.

McCarty, Clifford. *Bogey – The Films of Humphrey Bogart.* New York: The Citadel Press, 1965.

McClelland, Doug. *The Golden Age of "B" Movies.* New York: Bonanza Books, 1981.
— *Hollywood on Hollywood.* Boston: Faber and Faber, Inc., 1985.
— *Hollywood on Ronald Reagan.* Winchester, MA: Faber and Faber, Inc., 1983.

McClure, Arthur F. and Jones, Ken D. *Star Quality.* South Brunswick, NJ: A.S. Barnes, 1974.

McShine, Kynaston. *Andy Warhol – A Retrospective.* New York: Museum of Modern Art, 1989.

Medved, Harry. *The Fifty Worst Films of All Time.* New York: CBS Popular Library, 1978.

Medved, Harry and Michael. *Son of Golden Turkey Awards.* New York: Villard Books, 1986.

Michael, Paul, ed. *The American Movies.* New York: Garland Books, 1969.
— *Movie Greats.* New York: Garland Books, 1969.

Miller, Marc H. *Television's Impact on Contemporary Art.* Flushing, NY: The Queen's Museum, 1988.

Moldea, Dan E. *Dark Victory: Ronald Reagan, MCA, and the Mob.* New York: Viking, 1986.

Mordden, Ethan. *The Hollywood Studios.* New York: Alfred A. Knopf, 1988.

Morella, Joe and Epstein, Edward Z. *Jane Wyman.* New York: Delacorte Press, 1985.

Morella, Joe, Epstein, Edward Z. and Clark, Eleanor. *Those Great Movie Ads.* New Rochelle, NY: Arlington House, 1972.

Morella, Joe, Epstein, Edward Z. and Griggs, John. *The Films of World War II.* Secaucus, NJ: The Citadel Press, 1973.

Morris, Desmond. *Bodywatching – A Field Guide to the Human Species.* New York: Crown, 1985.

Morris, George. *Doris Day.* New York: Pyramid, 1976.
— *Errol Flynn.* New York: Pyramid, 1975.

Moyers, Bill. *The Secret Government – The Constitution in Crisis.* Cabin John, MD: Seven Locks Press, 1988.

Murphy, Sen. George with Lasky, Victor. *"Say. . .Didn't You Used To Be George Murphy?"* Bartholomew House, Ltd., 1970.

Neal, Patricia with DeNeut, Richard. *As I Am – An Autobiography.* New York: Simon and Schuster, 1988.

Newfield, Jack and Barrett, Wayne. *City for Sale – Ed Koch and the Betrayal of New York.* New York: Harper and Row, 1988.

Newhouse, John. *War and Peace in the Nuclear Age.* New York: Alfred A. Knopf, 1988.

Nobel, Peter, ed. *Films of the Year 1955-56.* London: Express Books, 1956.
— *Picture Parade.* London: Burke Publishing Company Ltd., 1949.

O'Neill, Tip with Novak, William. *Man of the House.* New York: Random House, 1987.

Orriss, Bruce W. *When Hollywood Ruled the Skies.* Hawthorne, CA: Aero Associates, Inc., 1984.

Owens, Bill. *Suburbia.* San Francisco: Straight Arrow Books, 1973.

Papritz, Carew and Tremayne, Russ, eds. *Reagancomics.* Seattle: Khyber Press, 1984.

Parish, James Robert. *Hollywood's Great Love Teams.* New Rochelle, NY: Arlington House, 1974.
— *The Fox Girls.* New Rochelle, NY: Arlington House, 1971.

Parish, James Robert and Bowers, Ronald L. *The MGM Stock Company.* New Rochelle, NY: Arlington House, 1973.

Parish, James Robert and Leonard, William T. *Hollywood Players – The Thirties*. Carlstadt, NJ: Rainbow Books, 1976.

Parish, James Robert and Stanke, Don E. *The All-Americans*. Carlstadt, NJ: Rainbow Books, 1978.
— *The Forties Gals*. Westport, CT: Arlington House, 1980.
— *The Swashbucklers*. New Rochelle, NY: Arlington House, 1976.

Pearman, Phil, ed. *Dear Editor: Letters to Time Magazine, 1923-1984*. Salem, NH: Salem House, 1985.

Peary, Danny. *Cult Movies*. New York: Delta, 1981.

Pickens, T. Boone. *Boone*. Boston: Houghton Mifflin Co., 1987.

Prindle, David F. *The Politics of Glamour*. Madison: The University of Wisconsin, 1988.

Quinlan, David. *Quinlan's Illustrated Directory of Film Stars*. New York: Hippocrene Books, Inc., 1986.

Quirk, Lawrence J. *Claudette Colbert – An Illustrated Biography*. New York: Crown Pub., Inc., 1985.
— *The Great Romantic Films*. Secaucus, NJ: The Citadel Press, 1974.
— *Jane Wyman. The Actress and the Woman*. New York: Dembner Books, 1986.

Rainsberger, Todd. *James Wong Howe Cinematographer*. San Diego: A.S. Barnes, 1981.

Ratcliff, Carter. *Komar and Melamid*. New York: Abbeville Press, 1988.

Regan, Donald T. *For the Record*. New York: Harcourt, Brace, Jovanovich, 1988.

Richards, Norman V. *Cowboy Movies*. Greenwich, CT: Bison Books Corp., 1984.

Riese, Randall, Hitchens, Neal. *The Unabridged Marilyn – Her Life from A to Z*. New York: Congdon and Weed, Inc., 1987.

Ringgold, Gene. *The Films of Bette Davis*. New York: The Citadel Press, 1966.

Robbins, Jhan. *Everybody's Man – A Biography of Jimmy Stewart*. New York: G.P. Putnam's Sons, 1985.

Robinson, L.T.A. Ltd., eds. *The Film Show Annual, 1955*. London: L.T.A. Robinson, Ltd.

Rogin, Michael Paul. *Ronald Reagan, the Movie*. Berkeley: University of California Press, 1987.

Rosebush, James S. *First Lady, Public Wife*. Lanham, MD: Madison Books, 1987.

Rothel, David. *The Great Show Business Animals*. San Diego: A.S. Barnes, 1980.

Ryan, Michael and Kellner, Douglas. *Cinema Politica: The Politics and Ideology of Contemporary Hollywood Film*. Bloomington, IN: Indiana University Press, 1988.

St. Johns, Adela Rogers. *Love, Laughter and Tears*. Garden City, NY: Doubleday and Co., Inc., 1978.

Scagnetti, Jack. *Movie Stars in Bathtubs*. Middle Village, NY: Jonathan David Publishers, Inc., 1975.

Schafer, Kermit. *Blooper Tube*. New York: Crown Publishers, Inc., 1979.

Schary, Dore and Palmer, Charles. *Case History of a Movie*. New York: Random House, 1950.

Scott, Walter. *Personality Parade*. New York: Grosset and Dunlap, Inc., 1971.

Seagrave, Sterling. *The Marcos Dynasty*. New York: Harper and Row, 1988.

Sennett, Ted. *The Movie Buff's Book*. New York: Pyramid, 1975.
— *Warner Brothers Presents*. New York: Castle Books, Inc., 1971.

Settel, Irving and Laas, William. *A Pictorial History of Television*. New York: Grosset and Dunlap, Inc., 1969.

Shields, Mark. *On the Campaign Trail*. Chapel Hill, NC: Algonquin Books, 1985.

Shipman, David with preface by Bergman, Ingmar. *The Story of Cinema*. New York: St. Martin's Press, 1982.

Shulman, Arthur and Youman, Roger. *How Sweet It Was*. New York: Bonanza Books, 1966.

Silverstein, Shel. *Playboy's Teevee Jeebies*. Chicago: Playboy Press, 1963.

Sinatra, Nancy. *Frank Sinatra My Father*. Garden City, NY: Doubleday and Co., Inc., 1985.

Slosser, Bob. *Reagan Inside Out*. Waco, Texas: World Books, 1984.

Smith, David and Gebbie, Melinda. *Reagan for Beginners*. London: Writers and Readers, 1984.

Smith, Ella. *Starring Miss Barbara Stanwyck*. New York: Crown, 1974.

Smith, George H. *Who Is Ronald Reagan?* New York: Pyramid Books, 1968.

Smith, Hedrick, ed. *Reagan the Man, the President.* New York: Macmillan, 1980.

Speakes, Larry. *Speaking Out.* New York: Charles Scribner's Sons, 1988.

Spears, Jack. *Hollywood: The Golden Era.* South Brunswick, NJ: A.S. Barnes, 1971.

Spina, Tony. *On Assignment – Projects in Photojournalism.* New York: Amphoto/ Watson-Guptill, 1982.

Springer, John. *Forgotten Films To Remember.* Secaucus, NJ: The Citadel Press, 1980.

Stacy, Jan and Syvertsen, Ryder. *The Great Book of Movie Monsters.* Bromley: Columbus Books, 1983.

Stockman, David A. *The Triumph of Politics.* New York: Harper and Row, 1986.

Summers, Anthony. *Goddess – The Secret Lives of Marilyn Monroe.* New York: Macmillan, 1985.

Thomas, Bob. *Golden Boy – The Untold Story of William Holden.* New York: St. Martin's Press, 1983.
— *The Heart of Hollywood.* Los Angeles: Price/Stern/Sloan, 1971.

Thomas, Tony. *The Films of Olivia deHavilland.* Secaucus, NJ: The Citadel Press, 1983.
— *The Films of Ronald Reagan.* Secaucus, NJ: The Citadel Press, 1980.
— *The Films of the Forties.* Secaucus, NJ: The Citadel Press, 1975.
— *Hollywood and the American Image.* Westport, CT: Arlington House, 1981.

Thomas, Tony, Behlmer, Rudy and McCarty, Clifford. *The Films of Errol Flynn.* New York: The Citadel Press, 1969.

Thompson, Howard, ed. *The New York Times Guide to Movies on TV.* Chicago: Quadrangle Books, 1970.

Tierney, Tom. *Nancy Reagan Fashion Paper Dolls.* Mineola, NY: Dover, 1983.
— *Ronald Reagan Paper Dolls.* Mineola, NY: Dover, 1984.

Trager, Oliver, ed. *The Iran-Contra Arms Scandal: Foreign Policy Disaster.* New York: Facts on File Pub., 1988.

Trudeau, G.B. *Talkin' About My G-G-Generation.* New York: Holt, Rinehart and Winston, 1988.

Trump, Donald J. with Schwartz, Tony. *Trump – The Art of the Deal.* New York: Random House, 1987.

Turner, Lana. *Lana – The Lady, the Legend, the Truth.* New York: E.P. Dutton, 1982.

Turner, Peter, ed. *American Images: Photography 1945-1980.* Middlesex, Eng.: Penguin Books, 1985.

Tuska, Jon. *The American West in Film.* Lincoln: University of Nebraska Press, 1988.

Ullmann, Owen. *Stockman – The Man, the Myth, the Future.* New York: Donald A. Fine, Inc., 1986.

Vance, Malcolm Frederick. *The Movie Quiz Book.* New York: Paperback Library, 1970.

Vermilye, Jerry. *Barbara Stanwyck.* New York: Pyramid, 1975.

Viguerie, Richard A. *The New Right: We're Ready To Lead.* Falls Church, VA: The Viguerie Co., 1981.

von Damm, Helene. *At Reagan's Side.* New York: Doubleday, 1988.

Von Hoffman, Nicholas. *Citizen Cohn.* New York: Doubleday, 1988.

Vonnegut, Kurt, introduction. *Paul Davis – Faces.* New York: Friendly Press, Inc., 1985.

Voss, Frederick S. *Man of the Year – A TIME Honored Tradition.* Washington, DC: National Portrait Gallery, Smithsonian Institution Press, 1987.

Wallace, Chris. *First Lady – A Portrait of Nancy Reagan.* New York: St. Martin's Press, 1986.

Wallis, Hal and Higham, Charles. *Starmaker.* New York: Macmillan, 1980.

Warman, Eric, ed. *Preview 1955.* London: Andrew Dakers Ltd., 1955.

Wead, Doug and Wead, Bill. *Reagan in Pursuit of the Presidency – 1980.* Plainfield, NJ: Haven Books, 1980.

Weldon, Michael. *The Psychotronic Encyclopedia of Film.* New York: Ballantine Books, 1983.

Wilk, Max. *Every Day's a Matinee.* New York: W.W. Norton and Co., Inc., 1975.

Wilkerson, Tichi and Borie, Marcia. *Hollywood Legends – The Golden Years of The Hollywood Reporter.* Los Angeles: Tale Weaver Pub., 1988.

Willis, Garry. *Reagan's America – Innocents at Home.* Garden City, NY: Doubleday, 1987.

Wilson, Arthur. *The Warner Bros. Golden Anniversary Book.* New York: Dell, 1973.

Wilson, Ivy Crane, ed. *Hollywood Album, 1948, 1949, 1952.* London: Sampson, Low, Marston and Co. Ltd. (1948 number republished in 1980 as *Hollywood in the 1940s.*)

Windeler, Robert. *The Films of Shirley Temple.* Secaucus, NJ: The Citadel Press, 1978.

Winship, Michael. *Television.* New York: Random House, 1988.

World Film Publications Ltd., eds. *Preview, 1948, 1949, 1950.* London: World Film Pub. Ltd.

Young, Christopher. *The Films of Doris Day.* Secaucus, NJ: The Citadel Press, 1977.

Zolotow, Maurice. *Shooting Star – A Biography of John Wayne.* New York: Simon and Schuster, 1974.

Primary Source Bibliography

Davis, Patti with Foster, Maureen Strange. *Home Front.* New York: Crown, 1986.

Reagan, Maureen with Herrmann, Dorothy. *First Father, First Daughter: A Memoir.* New York: Little, Brown & Co., 1989.

Reagan, Michael with Hyams, Joe. *On the Outside Looking In.* New York: Zebra, 1988.

Reagan, Nancy with Libby, Bill. *Nancy.* New York: William Morrow and Co., 1980.

Reagan, Ronald. *The Creative Story.* New York: Devin-Adair Co., 1968.
— *Grinning with the Gipper – A Celebration of the Wit, Wisdom, and Wisecracks of Ronald Reagan.* Eds., Denton, James S. and Schweizer, Peter. New York: Morgan Entrekin/Atlantic Monthly, 1988.
— *National Security Strategy of the United States.* Elmsford, NY: Pergamon Books, 1988.
— *Public Papers of the Presidents of the United States: Ronald Reagan, 1981-1985.* Washington, DC: United States Government Printing Office, 1982-1986.
— *Reagan on Cuba: Selected Statements by the President.* Foreword by Bush, George. Washington, DC: Cuban American National Foundation, 1986.
— *Ronald Reagan Talks to America.* Greenwich, CT: Devin-Adair Pub., Inc., 1982.
— *A Time for Choosing: The Speeches of Ronald Reagan.* Ed., Balitzer, Alfred. Washington, DC: Regnery Gateway, Inc., 1983.
— "How To Make Yourself Important." *Photoplay,* 1942: 21-3:44 (Aug.).
— "Horses Are My Hobby." *Hollywood Album,* 1948: 13-15.
— "It's More Than a Jungle." *Preview,* 1955: 44-46.

Reagan, Ronald with Hobbs, Charles D. *Ronald Reagan's Call to Action.* New York: Warner Books, 1976.

Reagan, Ronald with Hubler, Richard G. *Where's the Rest of Me?* New York: Duell, Sloan and Pearce, 1965.

Introductions for the following publications: Crane, Philip M. (*Surrender in Panama: The Case Against the Treaty*) 1978, Heyden, Richard S. and Despont, Thierry W. (*Restoring the Statue of Liberty*) 1986, Jagt, Guy V. (*A Country Worth Saving*) 1984, Kampelman, Max M. (*Three Years at the East-West Divide*) 1983, McDonald, Forrest (*Liberty's Five Flags*) 1988, Preiss, Byron, ed. (*Constitution*) 1987, Thatcher Margaret (*In Defense of Freedom*) 1987, Varghese, Roy A., ed. (*The Intellectuals Speak Out About God*) 1984, Viorst, Milton, ed. (*Making a Difference: The Peace Corps at Twenty-Five*) 1986.

George Washington	1789-1797
John Adams	1797-1801
Thomas Jefferson	1801-1809
James Madison	1809-1817
James Monroe	1817-1825
John Quincy Adams	1825-1829
Andrew Jackson	1829-1837
Martin Van Buren	1837-1841
William Henry Harrison	1841
John Tyler	1841-1845
James K. Polk	1845-1849
Zachary Taylor	1849-1850

Millard Fillmore	1850-1853
Franklin Pierce	1853-1857
James Buchanan	1857-1861
Abraham Lincoln	1861-1865
Andrew Johnson	1865-1869
Ulysses S. Grant	1869-1877
Rutherford B. Hayes	1877-1881
James A. Garfield	1881
Chester A. Arthur	1881-1885
Grover Cleveland	1885-1889
Benjamin Harrison	1889-1893
Grover Cleveland	1893-1897
William McKinley	1897-1901

Theodore Roosevelt	1901-1909
William H. Taft	1909-1913
Woodrow Wilson	1913-1921
Warren G. Harding	1921-1923
Calvin Coolidge	1923-1929
Herbert C. Hoover	1929-1933
Franklin D. Roosevelt	1933-1945
Harry S Truman	1945-1953
Dwight D. Eisenhower	1953-1961
John F. Kennedy	1961-1963
Lyndon B. Johnson	1963-1969
Richard M. Nixon	1969-1974
Gerald R. Ford	1974-1977
James E. Carter	1977-1981
Ronald Reagan	1981-1989
George Bush	1989-

C R E D I T S

Gallery Staff

Robert P. Metzger, Director

Cynthia A. Peltier, Assistant to the Director

Photographs

Principal photographer: Debra Cook

Credits

AIDS Coalition To Unleash Power

American Postcard Company

Artists Poster Committee

Ed Barber

Tom Car

Chesterfield Cigarettes

Eva Cockroft

Columbia Pictures

D M

D. James Dee

Donnelly / Colt

eeva-inkeri

Elvehjem Museum of Art

Michael Evans, SYGMA

Michael von Graffenreid

Jeff Kyler

Liz Loring

Michele Maier

Robert E. Mates

Leon McFadden

Metro-Goldwyn-Mayer

National Portrait Gallery,
  Smithsonian Institution

NBC TV

Elizabeth O'Neill

Paramount

Eric Pollitzer

Radio-Keith-Orpheum

Adam Reich

Udo Reuschling

Rosalyn Richards

Fred Scruton

Sharp Calculators

Jennifer Steinbrook

Swing Time Advertising

Turner Entertainment Co.

United Artists

Universal-International

Universal Pictures

Warner Brothers

Weiss Global Enterprises

143

INDEX OF ARTISTS